THE
ONLY
WOMAN

THE
ONLY
WOMAN

IMMY HUMES

INTRODUCTION

I got hooked by the artists, those beguiling group portrait photographs of a school, a movement, a bunch of brilliant friends and rivals. The one that first really struck me showed radical filmmaker Shirley Clarke celebrating her first feature in 1961. She stands, glass in hand, the only woman among twenty-two well-wishing men who fill the frame: her cast, crew, and backers. To me, it spoke volumes about this person often described as "the only woman filmmaker" of her time. Why her and *only* her? What does her oniness mean? I got a little fixated.

Other photos of Clarke in the sixties, looking quite fabulous as the only woman among many male filmmakers, turned up easily enough (including the one in this book), reawakening old familiar questions and feelings about women's integration, the long persistence and slow erosion of a man's world—indeed many, many men's worlds. And for me, a documentary filmmaker gazing at the pictures, I found myself embarrassed by my fangirl response: "You go, girl!" And then, knowing that working in a man's world was going to get harder for her, a more protective "Watch out, Shirley!"

Those photos were summoning others, ringing the bells of memory: "I've seen this before." Yes!—the shot in *Life* magazine of famous Abstract Expressionists and—there!—a woman I'd never heard of, sticking out at the top with her shiny leather handbag. The bells kept ringing: "What else? Who else?" As you will see, once you start to look for the Only Woman, she is easy to find—in the Bauhaus lineup, the Leo Castelli Gallery's artists in the 1980s, at the Algonquin Round Table.

65TH CANNES FILM FESTIVAL. EVEN IN 2012, THIS LINEUP OF FILM DIRECTORS STILL SEEMED NORMAL AND NOT LIKE THE LINE FOR THE MEN'S ROOM.
Cannes, France
2012

She was easy to find, and the pictures were at least vaguely familiar: iconic, canonical representations of the artists of the twentieth century. She was almost always an artist among artists, though often much less famous, sometimes forgotten.

Painters, writers, filmmakers, all these men with one woman—artists clearly had a thing for it! But then it turned out that scientists did too. And lawyers. And educators. And—you name it. I wasn't surprised that when those bearded, pot-smoking, patriarchal bad boys known as the Beat Generation were photographed, the group was all male—or all male with a single woman, be she infiltrator or cherry on top. But the American Society of Sugar Beet Technologists too?

One day I was looking at older and more ordinary pictures, trawling through soporific archives, as I like to do, pondering how a huge percentage of the photographic records of Western culture is incredibly boring: a gazillion large groups of formally dressed, formally arranged men, facing the camera.

Class pictures from every imaginable school, associations, companies, offices, clubs, courts, government bodies, and political movements from the revolutionary to the regressive. Lest we forget the centuries of all-male public life, in the public records, every picture in this book would be surrounded by all-male ones (which, while certainly less common these days, are still not hard to find). It was easy to think that most of these group portraits will never be looked at again—they're that dull.

13TH INTERNATIONAL CONGRESS OF MEDICINE
Paris, France
1900

HYGIENE SECTION, 17TH INTERNATIONAL
CONGRESS OF MEDICINE
London, England, UK
1913

LONDON SCHOOL OF TROPICAL
MEDICINE, 71ST SESSION
London, England, UK
1923

But then—I woke up. There were so many Only Women here too! Yes, the overwhelming majority of the groups were all male, but it was uncanny how many women had snuck in, one at a time. Very rarely two, never three, but so many Onlys. I felt like I was playing "Where's Waldo?" or, rather, "Walda." The pleasure of spotting them, and then, most of all, the mystery of them: What was *she* doing there?

Consider these medical groups in Paris and London, in 1900, 1913, and 1923, each with an Only Woman. Almost every other class was all male. There was no official one-woman quota or a single woman's scholarship, for example. This felt like an unaccountably frequent phenomenon. It was older and more common than I expected, and it existed to a depth I couldn't explain. This Onliness was not only a thing, but a thing I didn't understand at all. It felt a little creepy.

Tokenism is the first thought that leapt to mind, but it wasn't that. Tokenism (of which more later) is a performance of inclusivity, and like any performance, it requires an audience, at least an imaginary one. A group that takes in a token, a single other, is wishing to demonstrate or pretend that it is inclusive of that otherness the token represents. But most of these groups did not yet feel any pressure to open their doors to the excluded others. This was something else, something older.

One clue arrived with the discovery of one of my very favorite photos: a young lady standing with a graduating class of fine young men at the US Naval Academy in 1894. She wasn't a first woman classmate and was also pre-

CONGRESSWOMAN JEANNETTE
RANKIN WITH HER COLLEAGUES
FROM THE 65TH US CONGRESS
Washington, D.C, USA
1918.

tokenism. She is in the position of honor but looks a tad mortified. The original caption reads only "Class with Mascot." Mascot? A token is an "other" who is falsely called a member, but a mascot? A mascot is an "other" appointed by the group for fun, or luck, or encouragement; the word first came into the English language as the name of a virgin who magically brought good fortune to men.

It dawned on me that *men must like it.* It must have been a constellation that pleases, consciously or not. Some of the women liked it too,

of course, because as much as the Onlys may suffer—and many do, a lot—for some sometimes there are also the pleasures of egoism, erotic thrill, adventure, and gratitude for being able to live—in a way—like men. Or at least among them.

Food writer Gael Greene wrote in 1974, "I have never minded being the only woman at the party. Actually . . . confession-time . . . I have loved it. I remember one stirring moment at a wine tasting. I entered. Twenty-two men stood up. I sat down with a pleasing vision of what life

must have been like in one of my previous incarnations when, I am convinced, I was Elizabeth of England." [01] (Now that we are confessing, I admit that, for my fiftieth birthday, I invited twelve men to dinner and sat at the head of the table. It was fun.)

By the time I had culled hundreds of examples of the Only Woman phenomenon, many epithets were buzzing around in my mind: "one of the boys," "a man's woman," "a hidden figure," "a man in disguise," "disguised as a man," "queen bee," "figurehead," "sore thumb," and "stowa-

↑

way." The women were infinite, various, often mysterious. But, in examining the pictures, I could see more categories emerge, ways to become an Only Woman, in addition to the Mascots.

First of all, the *Firsts*. They are everywhere. In every institution, association, university, and court, in every country, district, and town, first women pop up. And Firsts, unlike Mascots, can have a very tough time. As the stories in this book show, it is common for Firsts to face ongoing male hostility. Many quit; many are forced out. A favorite First resides in this long, skinny 1918 photo of US Congress, with Jeannette Rankin, the *first-ever congress-woman*, sitting smack in the middle of the men.

A First implies sequence, which can be mislead-ing because many Firsts remain Onlys for such a long time. A First should have a superscript number to indicate how long she remained an Only. Often enough, the first woman is less a First and more the exception who proves the rule (the rule being that women do not belong here). Exceptions are paragons, superhumans like Marie Curie, who remained an Only for decades. Sometimes the genius required to become the First may end up discouraging others from following close behind. Who, after all, could follow Curie? (Her daughter, in fact, was the next woman to win a Nobel Prize in science, twenty-five years later.)

Another category of Only Women that we see in these photographs are just women doing their jobs, the highly gendered jobs that first brought them into the labor market and public life: cook, nurse, singer, actress, model, sex symbol, sex worker, servant, and assistant.

SMURFETTE WITH OTHER CHARACTERS FROM THE SMURFS
Created by Peyo
1966 (first appearance of Smurfette)

LADY BRENDA HALE, THE FIRST WOMAN JUSTICE
ON THE UK SUPREME COURT
London, England, UK
2010

The occupations were often at least originally body based, providing something necessary that men could not: the nurse began as someone nursing a baby; the soprano uses the instrument of her body to produce her uniquely female sounds. The pictures here show how those jobs served as passes into the all-male world: the secretary in the office, the model in the painting class.

Another smaller category are those who were born or married into it: they became an Only Woman because they were a wife or a daughter: Empress Cixi, Diana Spencer, Mary Morris, and Benazir Bhutto were stepping into the family business.

And then there is the Token, the category that first leaps to the modern mind when thinking about social onliness. Tokenism is lying, phony inclusion: appearing to invite the other in while in fact continuing to exclude. Tokenism can show in a conviction that only one of an excluded type of person is actually necessary. Tina Fey said in 2018, "When I first started out, female comedy writers were treated a little bit like cappuccino machines in that if you try to hire a few more between seasons, people will look at you like, 'But we have one. It's you. We have one.' And God forbid, the one you have is a little bit broken because it's like, 'Oh, no, you know, we had one before and it didn't work and we got rid of it.'" [02]

The Token contains the all. "The Smurfette Principle," a revelatory short essay by journalist and feminist Katha Pollitt from 1991, [03] gets at an aspect of tokenism that, while all too familiar, can also get mentally weird. The popular comic book *Smurfs* are little blue creatures, each named according to an occupation or personal quality:

LE JUGEMENT DE JEANNE D'ARC
Antony Serres
1867

FAY WRAY IN A STILL FROM
THE WEDDING MARCH
Directed by Erich von Stroheim
1928

MONICA VITTI IN A STILL
FROM *L'AVVENTURA*
Directed by Michelangelo Antonioni
1960

Carpenter Smurf, Fireman Smurf, Wanker Smurf, whatever. And then there is—Smurfette. The one and only female in the species, with her adorable Minnie Mouse bows and shoes; she was one, and so she was all. She contained multitudes: every single girl was represented by *the* girl. This is the mystical aspect of tokenism, whereby half the human race becomes one individual. Once familiar with the Smurfette principle, you cannot see movie posters or rock and roll bands the same way. *Star Wars, Seinfeld, Succession*—Smurfette is everywhere. She may *finally* be going out of style, but we've thought that before.

Literature, myth, art, and commerce, all the realms of invention and persuasion—including porn—are saturated with images of the one woman in a man's world, from Eve to Joan of Arc to Princess Leia. This collection sticks to "real life"—photographs of women in institutional, organizational, political, or social settings—and leaves aside paintings and movie stills. But all those other invented sisters can be heard, if only from the wings, in ghostly dialogue with the flesh-and-blood women in this book. This book is, essentially, a study of power, as seen in one hundred photographs of groups

of grown men—artists, workers, musicians, dentists, lawyers—with only one single woman. Spanning more than a century and a half, from 1862 to 2020, the photos were taken in the United States, the United Kingdom, Mexico, France, Peru, Pakistan, and fourteen other countries. They capture moments along a wide, slow current of change. Each photo offers forensic evidence of patriarchy on parade, along with all the other forces of domination.

GLORIA RICHARDSON AND OTHER CIVIL RIGHTS LEADERS
MEETING WITH ATTORNEY GENERAL ROBERT F. KENNEDY
Washington, DC, USA
1963

JE NE VOIS PAS LA [FEMME] CACHÉE
DANS LA FORÊT
René Magritte
1929

While collecting, for a long time I was bewitched by the "class photos," the deliberate self-presentations to the camera. I like these formal social selfies, the studied ways the group models itself. But examples from photojournalism began to demand inclusion; they are a different but complementary kettle of (male) fish, and some swam their way in, including irresistible pictures of lone women in street protests over time. The only photos ruled out altogether were those that pictured random configurations (a contemporary street scene) or family groups (a sister among her brothers), in which the fact of one woman among many men was not meaningful. And, to keep it honest, a certain rules-bound literalism was necessary: no little extra women in the background and no cropping either.

Against this wild variety of time, place, occupations, and cultures is a repetitive counterpoint of sameness. The same ludicrous constellation of many men, one woman, over and over again. That tension between repetition and particularity is one of the peculiar pleasures of looking at the pictures as a group.

These one hundred favorites are an idiosyncratic selection that does not aim to be representative or rigorous, scholarly, or political. I'd like to think that someone else will write those books, because I'm not a social scientist or a scholar. I'm more of a procrastinating storyteller, a documentarian who fell into a groove and kept making more and more personal and historical connections. My instinct was to want to hear the voices of the women; the silence of the stills is so frustrating and yet attractive too. Also, I wanted to share them, to discover if other people, especially women, would find them interesting too.

THE ONLY WOMAN

ANNA SEARCY

Medical Student
Columbia, Missouri, USA
1897

Searcy appears with her hat, her first-year classmates, professors, and "Bones," as he was identified in the *Savitar* yearbook of the University of Missouri School of Medicine. She definitely looks like "the odd man out"; among the bare-headed men in their starched collars, she wears that loopy zigzag of a hat, like a manic thought bubble, and a facial expression just as memorable.

The caption identified her as "class secretary," and it was only recently that she was recognized as, in fact, the first woman to enter the school and graduate as a doctor. The discovery was made thanks to the sleuthing of Dr. Elizabeth Garrett, who embarked on a quest to learn the life stories of her alma mater's first women graduates. Their life stories—as much as Garrett has been able to rescue from oblivion—are remarkable; she's discovered intense community service, advanced basketball skills, adventures from Puerto Rico to Berlin, and notably long lives. One who practiced till ninety-four said she had no reason to retire, she just told her patients to *knock louder.*

Garrett found that Searcy was an orphan, who was sent to college by a charity fund. The young woman believed that her lucky break was the answer to years of fervent prayer. She was already in her thirties by the time she entered the medical school, which was then under a dean (the gentleman with the white beard) who supported women in medicine. It was a demanding course: of her entering class of twenty-five, mostly boys just out of high school, she was one of only four to graduate. She went on to a small-town practice and was noted for her generous support of a charitable educational fund. [04]

The Missouri Medical School in 2018 initiated a special annual award in Searcy's name. The first winner was Dr. Garrett, and the design of the award itself is an abstract homage to Anna Searcy's fabulous hat.

HEDDA STERNE

Artist
New York, New York, USA
1951

Most of the painters here are even more famous than the photo—Jackson Pollock, Mark Rothko, and Willem de Kooning among them. But the only woman is not, even though it is her presence and position—"a feather in the hat," as she put it—that make the image so arresting. In fact, Sterne said that the photo was "probably the worst thing that happened to me" since "I am known more for that darn photo than for eighty years of work." But she added, "If I had an ego, it would bother me." [05]

Sterne was anti-ego, anti-logo, almost anti–Abstract Expressionist, which is how most of these men came to be described. Her artwork was different, idiosyncratic, and ever changing: Surrealist autocollage, New York in spray paint, an intricate floor journal, and other incarnations. Her whole self-conception was different too: "I am only one small speck (hardly an atom) in the uninterrupted flux of the world around me." [06]

The artists were protesting the Metropolitan Museum of Art's retrograde attitudes about "advanced art," i.e., Abstraction. The fight was front-page news; it was about a revolution in perception, the meaning of modern art, postwar American cultural muscle. The men, who feared being dismissed as Bohemians or sellouts, were trying to look respectable, "like bankers." It's notable how conservative these white patriarchal revolutionaries look now.

Sterne recollected, "When we arrived, each chair had a name on it. But there was no chair for me. It wasn't deliberate, though, and they found something for me to stand on, in the back." However, the men "were very furious that I was in it because they all were sufficiently macho to think that the presence of a woman took away from the seriousness of it all." [07]

"The guys would say, 'Oh, you are one of us!' or 'You paint just like a man.' That was supposed to make me die with being pleased." [08]

After she married a fellow Romanian immigrant, the artist Saul Steinberg, she resisted the role of artist's wife but said, "In the apartment, there was never something of mine on the wall. And lots of people, our friends, didn't know I was Hedda Sterne." [09]

First row, seated L–R:
THEODOROS STAMOS, JIMMY ERNST, BARNETT NEWMAN, JAMES BROOKS, and MARK ROTHKO.

Second row, L–R:
RICHARD POUSETTE-DART, WILLIAM BAZIOTES, JACKSON POLLOCK, CLYFFORD STILL, ROBERT MOTHERWELL, and BRADLEY WALKER TOMLIN.

Third row, L–R:
WILLEM DE KOONING, ADOLPH GOTTLIEB, AD REINHARDT, and HEDDA STERNE.

LEONA WOODS

Physicist
Chicago, Illinois, USA
1946

At twenty-three, Woods helped build the first nuclear reactor and the atom bomb. In a later oral history, the *Voices of the Manhattan Project*, an interviewer asked her if "anybody took note of the fact that you were a woman. Did you have any problems . . . or were you treated differently?" She replied, "That's a dumb thing to say!" and changed the subject. [10] She didn't like to talk about being the only woman. She found it uninteresting.

She was a prodigy who graduated from the University of Chicago in chemistry at nineteen. She asked Nobel laureate James Franck to accept her as his graduate student. He agreed but told her that his own advisor had said to him:

"You are a Jew; you will starve to death." And he echoed to her: "You are a woman, and you will starve to death." [11] She chose another advisor.

In December 1942, she was the only woman among the forty-nine scientists and workers who witnessed Chicago Pile-1—the world's first controlled, self-sustaining nuclear chain reaction—going critical. Four years later, fifteen of those participants were reunited here on the steps of Eckhart Hall at the University of Chicago.

First row, L–R:
ENRICO FERMI, WALTER ZINN, ALBERT WATTENBERG, and HERBERT ANDERSON.

Second row, L–R:
HAROLD AGNEW, WILLIAM STURM, HAROLD LICHTENBERGER, LEONA WOODS, and LEÓ SZILÁRD.

Third row, L–R:
NORMAN HILBERRY, SAMUEL ALLISON, THOMAS BRILL, ROBERT NOBLES, WARREN NYER, and MARVIN WILKENING.

MARIE CURIE

Physicist and Chemist
Brussels, Belgium
1911

Curie, head in hand, is pictured here at the first of the Solvay Conferences, the preeminent gatherings in Belgium that came to define much of twentieth-century physics and chemistry. It was the year she won her second Nobel Prize. Curie, who discovered radioactivity, was an Only Woman par excellence. The discoverer of radioactivity, she held the position of Only and First for a long time: the first woman to get a PhD in France, the first woman to win a Nobel Prize, the first person to win two Nobel Prizes. All six of the first Solvay Conference photographs immortalize her as the Only Woman. The last time there was only one woman at Solvay was in 1969, fifty-eight years after the first.

Curie's exceptional genius and devotion to science is legendary, and the stories of the discrimination she endured and defied are toe curling. While her husband, Pierre, was promoted to a professorship at the Sorbonne, she was not. In 1910 the all-male membership of the French Academy of Sciences voted not to admit her. Still all male in 1951, the academy did the same thing to her Nobelist daughter, Irène Joliot-Curie.

Such repetition forces us to pay more attention to the meaning of Firsts. We tend to think of Firsts as opening a door for a stream of followers, but often they are not "followable" anytime soon.

Historian Julie Des Jardins posits a "Curie complex," a paradoxical phenomenon encountered by women in science in the wake of Curie's genius, difficulties, and self-abnegation. Her exceptionalism at once inspires and discourages. Her exceptionalism at once inspires and discourages; while her towering example has encouraged women to enter science, it can also lead them (and society at large) to uphold the prodigious standards of the Firsts—and thus judge themselves inadequate. [12]

In this way, the Great Exception version of the Only Woman can become a kind of self-fulfilling prophecy. The greater the genius of the trailblazer, the harder it may be for mere mortals to follow. Permission to be average can sometimes be the ultimate privilege.

Seated, L–R: WALTHER NERNST, MARCEL BRILLOUIN, ERNEST SOLVAY, HENDRIK LORENTZ, EMIL WARBURG, JEAN BAPTISTE PERRIN, WILHELM WIEN, MARIE CURIE, HENRI POINCARÉ.

Standing, L–R: RICHARD GOLDSCHMIDT, MAX PLANCK, HEINRICH RUBENS, ARNOLD SOMMERFELD, FREDERICK LINDEMANN, MAURICE DE BROGLIE, MARTIN KNUDSEN, FRIEDRICH HASENÖHRL, GEORGES HOSTELET, ÉDOUARD HERZEN, JAMES H. JEANS, ERNEST RUTHERFORD, HEIKE KAMERLINGH ONNES, ALBERT EINSTEIN, PAUL LANGEVIN.

RITA LEVI-MONTALCINI

Neurobiologist
Vatican City, Italy
1986

There are some little girls who take one look at their mother's life and think, "not for me." One of them was Levi-Montalcini, the only woman among the Nobel Prize winners in science who were gathered here in the Vatican.

Levi-Montalcini was born in Turin, Italy, in 1909. Her father took a Victorian view of women's education: it should not go beyond finishing school, and she should graduate with a Mrs. However, the young girl convinced her father to let her study medicine, cramming years' worth of Greek, Latin, and mathematics into eight months so she could attend the University of Turin, where she graduated not with a husband but with the highest distinction in medicine and surgery, before beginning advanced studies in neurology and psychology.

The next man who tried to stand in her way was Mussolini, whose new "race laws" barred Jews from professional or academic careers. Kicked out of school, she went to Brussels to study, only to flee yet again when Germany was about to invade Belgium. Eventually, she returned to Turin and built a laboratory in her bedroom, fashioning scalpels from sewing needles, using an ophthalmologist's scissors, and watchmaker's forceps.

Inspired by an article by renowned embryologist Viktor Hamburger, she dissected chick embryos and studied their motor neurons under a microscope. She even took on an assistant, Giuseppe Levi, who had also been expelled from the university, and together they developed a theory that laid the foundation for the modern concept of nerve cell death as a part of normal development. As Jews, they couldn't publish in Italy, but their results in foreign journals caught the eye of Hamburger himself, who invited Levi-Montalcini to join him at Washington University in St. Louis. In 1948, soon after she arrived at Hamburger's laboratory, they noticed that a type of mouse tumor spurred nerve growth when implanted into chick embryos, and soon figured out the cause: a substance they named nerve growth factor (NGF), which biochemist Stanley Cohen was able to isolate. The 1986 Nobel Prize was awarded jointly to Levi-Montalcini and Cohen.

In 2001 she received one of Italy's highest honors when she became a "senator for life." At the age of ninety-seven, she held the deciding vote in the Italian parliament in a budget dispute, threatening to withdraw her support unless the government reversed its decision to cut science funding. The funding was reinstated, despite the opposition's attempts to silence her by mocking her age—or maybe because of it. To Levi-Montalcini, obstacles were motivating. "If I had not been discriminated against or had not suffered persecution, I would never have received the Nobel Prize." [13]

LUCILLE KALLEN

Television Comedy Writer
New York, New York, USA
1952

My idea of success was to be a boy—possibly because my brothers were my father's pride and joy, whereas he had to be introduced to me several times before he got it firmly planted in his mind that I was part of the family. [14]
—Lucille Kallen

Almost hidden here among the big guys, Kallen was best known for being the only woman in the legendary writers' room of *Your Show of Shows*—a variety show starring Sid Caesar and Imogene Coca—from 1950 to 1954. The writers' room was home of the best-known American postwar comic minds. In a 1998 interview, Kallen recounted what she had to do to make herself heard among such a noisy and "ruthless" group—"I finally resorted to standing up on the couch and waving a red kerchief to get attention"—but explained that "at the time, I wasn't aware of it," as she "was so stunned by the enormous good fortune of this situation, I mean I was on the most important and popular television show." [15]
It wasn't until later that she came to see things differently.

"Subsequently, I said, What an idiot! Of course there was always, underneath, this feeling that I was a woman. Bottom line is, you're a woman. It was clear to me that they had females divided up into certain categories. There were the Broads. Who were for fun things. And then there were the Wives. Who had another function. And I sort of didn't fit into anything," she remarked, with a laugh. [16]

Wives and broads, virgins and whores—that old categorical binary is fundamental to patriarchy. "Person" is a category of womanhood that Only Women like Kallen tried to establish.

SID CAESAR (standing, 3rd from L), MEL BROOKS (turned away, seated far L), MAX LIEBMAN (bowtie), <u>LUCILLE KALLEN</u>.

ELLEN WILKINSON

Politician
Harrogate, England, UK
1936

"Red Ellen," as she was called for both her hair color and her politics, was a First in so many ways it's hard to count. From a painfully poor family in northern England, she became a radical socialist, communist (for a time), feminist activist and leader, writer, member of Parliament, and cabinet minister. She never married or had children but was rumored to have a very active love life. (Her brother burned her papers after she died, so her privacy remains intact.)

In 1924 she became a member of Parliament, at a time when women were not allowed in the members' dining room, not to mention their bars and other sacrosanct spaces. Wilkinson was the first woman ever to attempt entry to the members' smoking room. She was stopped by a policeman at the door, who warned her that ladies were not allowed. She replied, "I am not a lady—I am a member of Parliament" and sailed ahead. [17]

She is seen here in her most famous incarnation: leader of the Jarrow March. Jarrow, one of the poorest towns in England, was in her district. It was devastated by unemployment in the Great Depression. Putting her experience organizing suffrage and other marches to work, she helped behind the scenes as the town chose two hundred men to march to London to demand work on behalf of the entire community. She camped and marched with the men as their member of Parliament and stalwart supporter for the thirty days it took. Here she is pictured at a rest stop with the marchers and their canine mascot.

UNKNOWN

Cowgirl
Unknown, USA
1910s–1920s

Almost no information about this photograph survives. It dates from the 1910s or 1920s, location and persons unknown. Hints to the identity of the crew, however, lie in their notably stylish clothing; the neatness of the fringed pants, shirts, and our lady's skirt, the matching hats and bandanas, and perhaps also their wearer's whiteness and anodyne good looks, announce that these are not work clothes but costumes, not ranch hands but performers.

Cowboy history expert Rich Slatta told us that, "No working cowboy would have worn such garb, but rodeo riders did. I would guess the time period is the 1920s, when men and women both competed in rodeos. During the 1930s, owing to the economic pressures of the Great Depression, men kicked women out of major rodeo events to cut down on the competition." [18] But the curators at the National Cowboy Museum disagree: "These are not cowboys or even rodeo cowboys. They are performers of some type and probably in a vaudeville show and not a Wild West show. Their hats and trousers are all wrong. In fact, the woman has the only truly Western-appearing hat." [19]

Cowboys were once real people—from the 1850s on, before the invention of barbed wire and the railroads cut up the great open spaces, huge herds of cattle were indeed driven over great distances in the American west by men of many ethnicities on horses. The rare women who actually worked cattle either led lives as men, or made the newspapers as astonishing exceptions who proved the rule that cowboy life was all-male.

The idea of the cowboy, however, soon began to outpace the real thing. The imaginary cowboy, icon of American masculinity, traveled the entire world. Actors and athletes, art, entertainment, and advertising, took over, long outlasting the actual workers. Cowgirls were an invention of the second, performing, cowboy era, and some did exceedingly well, from sharpshooter Annie Oakley to women working today. Historian Mary Lou LeCompte says women athletes were able to enter and shine in western shows long before other sports arenas: "Rodeo cowgirls were among America's pioneer professional athletes, achieving financial success and international acclaim." [20]

Those fringe-wearing, gun-toting, horse-riding women, who worked not cattle but an audience, found a way to fascinate by performing their own twist on the fantasy of masculinity, showing off their own dazzling shooting, riding, beauty, and costumes.

LAUFEY VALDIMARSDÓTTIR

School Student
Reykjavík, Iceland
1910

Valdimarsdóttir, here with her classmates at Reykjavík High School, was the first woman to graduate from secondary school in Iceland, a country that is now always a front-runner on lists of the most gender-equal societies in the world.

We might say that she inherited her position as an Only Woman and a First, since her mother, Bríet Bjarnhéðinsdóttir, was a famous feminist and powerhouse, who, even though she was denied formal education, became the first woman to publish a newspaper article (on women's rights), to lecture in public, to found a woman's magazine, to run for and win a seat on the city council, and to organize for suffrage. Her daughter went into that family business and then some.

The National Museum of Iceland tells us what became of the male students in the photo, who all grew up to take the important roles assigned to men of their social class: five doctors, three businessmen, a member of parliament, a Supreme Court judge, a writer, an editor, a banker, and a priest. But Valdimarsdóttir is identified as . . . a secretary. Though she did keep an office job in her brother's company, she also became the head of the Icelandic Women's Rights Association and worked in a number of ways and positions for labor rights of mothers and poor women. She was an art and animal lover and devoted her life to other women, especially to the cause of maternity pay for all single mothers.

She had health problems and died at age fifty-five in 1945, on a trip to Paris, a city she had longed to visit and where she said that she "saw life again with twenty eyes." [21]

COLETTE

Writer
Paris, France
1936

You do flatter yourself, you know, always imagining that you're the only one of your kind. [22]
—Colette

Colette spent a long lifetime fashioning herself as the Great Exception, a person unlike any before or since. In addition to being an original, and prolific writer, she was a compelling public figure. A bold seducer, lover of women and men, she reinvented herself often and celebrated her own many contradictions. She won acclaim for writing about women's lives and seems like the original liberated woman, but she despised feminism. "Suffragettes disgust me," she once said. "And if some women in France decide to imitate them, I hope that they will be made to understand that such behaviors are not appropriate in France. Do you know what suffragettes deserve? The whip and the harem."

She was a nonstop scandal from her early days in vaudeville. Many saw her as selfish, immoral, perhaps even criminal. In her forties, she flaunted a five-year sexual and romantic relationship with her stepson, which began when he was only sixteen. She was an abandoning mother, and the wife of a Jew who nevertheless published in anti-Semitic journals. And yet, here she is, as she was often seen in her later years, the sole woman at the very heart of the French cultural establishment: sitting on a jury with other luminaries. When she died in 1954, she was the first woman ever to receive a state funeral. She had made herself into a national monument, an embodiment of France.

GEORGE DUHAMEL (facing away, talking to) ANDRÉ MAUROIS. PAUL VALÉRY (wearing a bowtie and standing next to), COLETTE, POL NEVEUX (to the right of Valery), and FRANCOIS MAURIAC (second from left).

NATHALIE SARRAUTE

Writer
Paris, France
1959

These *nouveaux romanciers* (new novelists), assembled outside the publishing house Les Éditions de Minuit, are waiting for the last to arrive. Their legendary publisher, Jérôme Lindon, looks elegant, at least among this crew, but is nervously peering down the block; can he herd these avant-garde cats long enough to get a decent photo? As he feared, by the time the tardy writer showed up, Samuel Beckett had gotten tired of waiting.

The only woman is standing to Beckett's left, with her legs so tightly wound that she looks like she could fly straight up like a rubber band helicopter toy. Or is she planted, with patient irritation? Or maybe she is kind of hating them all? She certainly despised Beckett.

She was a Russian Jew, a well-off lawyer, married with three children, who almost never spoke of her terrifying years surviving World War II in France: the close calls, the precarious hiding places, forged papers (she became Nicole Sauvage), and a divorce to protect her husband from her Jewishness. Once, while laying low with her family in the countryside, she took Beckett in briefly, since he was also in danger—but she later sniffed, "The word grateful didn't seem to be in Beckett's vocabulary." [23]

Sarraute was almost one hundred when she died in 1999, after seven decades as a novelist, essayist, and dramatist. No sentimentalist, she was tough, smart, ambitious, and precise. She worked to win women the right to vote in France, which they didn't have when she published her first book, *Tropisms*, in 1939. She called it a novel but wanted it to be an entirely new kind of novel: no characters, no story, and trying to express real, almost-subconscious, moments in the human mind.

One of its short passages considers idle women, who sit in cafes and chat: "In the afternoon they went out together. . . . And they talked and talked, repeating the same things, going over them, then going over them again, from one side then from the other, kneading and kneading them, continually rolling between their fingers this unsatisfactory, mean substance that they had extracted from their lives (what they called "life," their domain), kneading it, pulling it, rolling it until it ceased to form anything between their fingers but a little pile, a little gray pellet." [24]

At eighty, she wrote her first best seller, a self-interrogating autobiography titled *Childhood*.

L–R: ALAIN ROBBE-GRILLET, CLAUDE SIMON, CLAUDE MAURIAC, JÉRÔME LINDON, ROBERT PINGET, SAMUEL BECKETT, NATHALIE SARRAUTE, and CLAUDE OLLIER.

MRS. FAIRFAX

Cook
Harrison's Landing, Virginia, USA
1862

Who is Mrs. Fairfax? She stands off to the side, a little out of focus, but commands the eye. The only woman among white men in uniform, Mrs. Fairfax gazes directly at the camera, hands folded in a posture of readiness and service, as the well-fed Yankee officers look off to some imagined horizon, a few weeks after a victory on the James River, near the first-ever plantation in Virginia.

Was she freshly emancipated from slavery, perhaps one of the many brave Black people in the South who fled behind Union lines seeking freedom? In this early period of the Civil War, the Union officially treated people who escaped as "contraband," property that, according to their rules of war, was to be returned to their Confederate enslavers. And not all the white men fighting on the Union side were in favor of abolition, including the commanding officer here. He would not have harbored a self-emancipated person, so it seems likely that Mrs. Fairfax was a freed woman before the war.

Black women in both the North and South struggled for survival during the war yet also found innumerable ways to fight for freedom. Pension claims and other evidence tell us that at least a few hundred managed to pose as men, successfully enlisting and fighting as soldiers.

An untold number also served officially and unofficially in traditionally female support jobs, as laundresses, cooks, and nurses. A woman's job often serves as a special back-stage pass to the world of men; when a cook or a nurse is needed, the gates of the man's world open to admit a necessary woman.

But the female workers of the war, especially Black women, were usually framed out. Of the many thousands of Civil War–era photographs, few show Black women. When they do appear, they are usually unnamed, like the three shadowy men in the background here. Fragments such as this image are precious to the growing number of scholars who are devoted to excavating Black women's buried wartime experience.

This photograph was a gift from one general (seated) to another. His handwritten caption identifies her as "Mrs. Fairfax", using an honorific that was denied Black women, and "Chief Cook and bottle washer," an old-fashioned way of saying she did everything and was indispensable. But her own truth remains silent.

Col Locke   Maj Monteith   Dr MᶜMillan   Capt MᶜQuaide   Col Norton   Mrs Fairfax

Maj Kirkland   Gen Porter   Head Quarters Fifth Army Corps   Capt Mason   Chief Cook & Bottle Washer

August 8ᵗʰ 1862   Harrison's Landing. James River. Va.

UNKNOWN

Student
Nashville, Tennessee, USA
1899

I constantly felt (as I suppose many an ambitious girl has felt) a thumping from within unanswered by any beckoning from without. [25]

— Anna J. Cooper, *A Voice from the South*, 1892

The unidentified female student here was, at the time, the only woman enrolled in the Academic Department at Roger Williams University in Nashville, pursuing a three-year college prep program in math and classics. Roger Williams offered two other programs: Ministry (all male) and Normal (teacher training, for both men and women). The school was one of scores of colleges established in the South for newly emancipated people, new institutions that were necessary because even after the abolition of slavery, most white colleges continued to refuse African Americans—and all women.

The first person to break the two-hundred-year white male monopoly on higher education in the United States was the beautifully named Alexander Lucius Twilight, who graduated from Middlebury College in 1823 and went on to become the first African-American state legislator. He was followed twenty years later by the first white woman, who graduated from a southern women's college that did not admit Black women—until—1968. The first Black woman to earn a bachelor's degree was Mary Jane Patterson, at Oberlin College in 1862.

These Firsts were followed slowly: by 1890, only 2,500 white women, 300 Black men, and 30 Black women had managed to overcome the obstacles to earning college degrees. The woman pictured here was on the long road to join them.

ANNA DE NOAILLES

Poet
Paris, France
1922

If God exists, I'd be the first to be told. [26]

—Anna de Noailles

A Romanian-Greek princess by birth and a French countess by marriage, de Noailles was an acclaimed poet and novelist with a brilliant career. She was a *salonière* who knew and was friendly with *le tout Paris* from the turn of the nineteenth century until her death in 1933.

Beautiful, charming, multilingual, and sickly most of her life, she was principally known as a writer of intense poetry. She was feminist in her assertion of female sexuality, materialist rather than religious, republican, pacifist, and a believer in women's suffrage. Scholar Catherine Perry writes, "de Noailles constructed an original poetic world view. Her work is best described as Dionysian—ecstatic, sensual, erotic, playful, sometimes violent, and always marked by a tragic undercurrent." [27]

De Noailles wrote about nature, love, illness, death, patriotism, and the downtrodden. Her books sold better than her friend Colette's, and she was the first woman to become a commander of the Legion of Honor in 1931.

In 1921 she won the Grand Prix of the Académie Française. Today her work is barely known.

She was close to Marcel Proust and Jean Cocteau, with whom she kept up a busy correspondence. Among her lovers were Maurice Barrès and Edmond Rostand. She was painted by Édouard Vuillard and sculpted by Auguste Rodin.

Apart from all that, this photograph is witness to the vastness of her range: here she is, sitting next to Albert Einstein, at a luncheon given in his honor when he came to Paris to lecture on the theory of relativity. With them are an international selection of distinguished scientists, statesmen, and scholars. Though Einstein was the guest of honor, de Noailles was the real attraction—an elegant and celebrated artist, a free spirit who made her own rules, an embodiment of the divine feminine.

Seated, L–R:
PAUL LANGEVIN, ALBERT EINSTEIN, <u>ANNA DE NOAILLES</u>, and PAUL PAINLEVÉ.

Standing, L–R:
THOMAS BARCLAY, LEO STRISOWER, PAUL APPELL, ÉMILE BOREL, and HENRI LICHTENBERGER.

VIRGINIA WRIGHT

Stick-up Artist
New York, New York, USA
1931

The "gun moll" entered pop and gangster culture in the 1920s and stayed. The term originally had Jewish roots: *gun* is not from firearms but the Yiddish word *gonif*, meaning thief. With *moll*, old slang for prostitute, it becomes "thief's whore." The gangster's side piece, the reckless and sexy Bonnie to Clyde, she flaunted her sexuality, courage, and hard-heartedness, but she was still always somebody's girl.

Wright, aliases Bobbie Bates and Billie Bates, is held here at a New York police station with ten men, all accused of "stick-ups." She is elegant in a long black Persian lamb coat, ruffled skirt, fabulous if unbuckled shoes, and marcelled bob. She does not look like anybody's moll. This looks more like the Bobbie Bates Gang than any other arrangement. The newspapers did, however, call her a "gun moll." [28]

Police claimed she and the men had confessed to more than a hundred robberies in the Brooklyn and Queens boroughs of New York. They were caught because the guys started shooting out windows in frustration when one robbery yielded only seven dollars. Wright's sentencing made the front page of the *New York Daily News* on February 7, 1931, which ran a fetching photo and the headline "Bad News", with a report that the "blonde gungirl" got three to six years. Many of the men drew sentences of up to thirty.

SIMONE KAHN BRETON

Gallerist
Paris, France
1924

I wish you to have, for seven days, as many sexes as you have fingers on your right hand. [29]
—Simone Kahn Breton, automatic sleep text, 1924

Kahn Breton was born into a prosperous Alsatian Jewish family, in the Peruvian jungle town of Iquitos, where her father was a rubber merchant. She studied literature and philosophy at the Sorbonne and quickly fell into the radical and subversive Surrealist movement. When she married André Breton in 1921, she assumed a central position in the group. She was vibrant, cultured, intelligent, and a true believer, yet also deferential to, and supportive of, the men. She is famous as a letter writer: her intense correspondence with her best friend and others is an extraordinary record of the events and aspirations of the movement.

Her position is perfectly expressed in this Man Ray photograph of the major Surrealist poets and artists gathered around her at her house in one of their sleep sessions of automatic writing.

The idea was to fall into a kind of trance state, to access the unconscious mind and speak a stream of uncensored words, a kind of hypnotic encounter with the self. (After about a year the sleep experiments were cancelled when Robert Desnos, still apparently in his sleep state, went after Paul Éluard with a kitchen knife.)

Kahn Breton was at once central, the gravitational core, the sun of the group; and yet also secretarial, supportive, embodying two aspects of the eternal feminine.

Foreground: <u>SIMONE KAHN BRETON</u>, ROBERT DESNOS, and JACQUES BARON.

Behind, L-R: MAX MORISE, ROGER VITRAC, JACQUES-ANDRÉ BOIFFARD, ANDRÉ BRETON, PAUL ÉLUARD, PIERRE NAVILLE, GIORGIO DE CHIRICO, and PHILIPPE SOUPAULT.

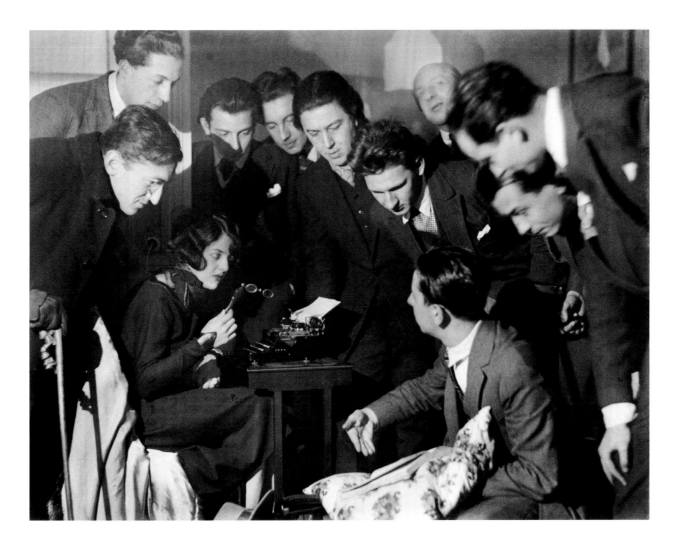

LIL HARDIN

Musician and Songwriter
Chicago, Illinois, USA
1923

In the early years of jazz, the few women performers were almost all singers; instrumentalists were exceedingly rare. Hardin was both—and more. Sent by her mother, a domestic worker, to Fisk University in Nashville to study music, Hardin ended up finding a job back home in Chicago demonstrating sheet music and wowing customers. By the time she was twenty, she was the hottest pianist in town, playing with different groups and writing songs.

The band pictured here includes a player on trombone newly arrived from New Orleans, none other than the young Louis Armstrong. After he and Hardin got married in 1924, she made the country boy over and pushed him to launch his own phenomenal career. She set up his Hot Five and Hot Seven bands, and together they made the first jazz recordings ever, including, when Louis let loose on "Heebie Jeebies," the first recording of scat.

Armstrong and Hardin eventually divorced but stayed friends for life. She continued a long, varied career performing in Europe and the United States, and her songs have been recorded by Ray Charles, Frank Sinatra, and Ringo Starr. She was exceptional on her own, but in cultural memory she is usually eclipsed by her husband's monumental genius and fame. In 1971, one month after Armstrong died, she was playing "St. Louis Blues" at a memorial concert for him when she collapsed at the piano and died herself.

L–R: HONORÉ DUTREY (trombone), BABY DODDS (drums), JOE KING OLIVER (trumpet), LOUIS ARMSTRONG (kneeling, trombone), LIL HARDIN (piano), WILLIAM "BILL" JOHNSON (banjo), and JOHNNY DODDS (clarinet).

ALICE CHALIFOUX

Harpist
Cleveland, Ohio, USA
1946

Symphony orchestras have been painfully slow to inte-
grate women but sometimes made an exception for the
harpist. The Vienna Philharmonic excluded women players
from full membership until 1997. That year it promoted its
harpist—who had been playing with them for twenty-six
years as an associate—to be its only female full member.
Ten years later it still had only one woman: the harpist who
replaced her.

Chalifoux, who joined the Cleveland Orchestra in 1931,
didn't seem to mind being for many years the only woman.
After retiring in 1974, she reminisced, "When we began
to get women in the orchestra in '43, the men would say,
'We have three women and Alice.' I had to be one of them
to avoid problems. On tour, we'd go to a bar and have
a high old time." [30]

Described in her obituary in Cleveland's newspaper *The
Plain Dealer* as "diminutive, salty-tongued, and beloved,"
Chalifoux was a promoter of women musicians and a
devoted teacher, keeping at it almost until her death at
one hundred years old. [31]

Even as women are steadily increasing their symphonic
participation, the gendering of instruments persists: a 2018
study of the world's top orchestras found that 94 percent
of harpists were women and 100 percent of trombonists
and tuba players were men.

ETHEL STARK

Violinist and Conductor
Montreal, Canada
c. 1946

This publicity photo of the Canadian Broadcasting Corporation's symphony orchestra does not have a typical PR vibe. Ethel Stark, the First Violinist and, indeed, most of the players behind her, look a little deflated. Perhaps Stark's posture was expressing how she felt about so often being the only woman in her classical music career.

She grew up in Montreal in a middle-class Jewish family. Her father, an insurance agent, played the violin. After years of rigorous music study, Stark managed to become a soloist and even a conductor, thanks to an iron determination and helpful early mentors. As she later reflected, hers was an exceptional experience: "It didn't matter how good a woman was, she didn't have a chance." [32]

She eventually got so fed up with being the Only that she did a full about-turn at the age of twenty-nine, founding an all-women's orchestra in 1940. She recruited forty players and founded the Montreal Women's Symphony Orchestra (MWSO). The biggest initial difficulty was to correct for the persistent gender segregation within the classical world by convincing pianists and violinists to suddenly become trombonists and tuba players. One violinist remembered that "she was a very fine musician who allowed no sloppiness to go unchallenged. If she heard wrongdoings, she could roar like a lion." [33]

The orchestra, which she conducted, was popular and successful, if financially fragile. It played New York's Carnegie Hall in 1947, marking a first for a Canadian symphony and for a female conductor. Stark and her collaborators kept the MWSO going for twenty years, and she herself had an extraordinary career as a guest conductor for major orchestras around the world. Meanwhile, many of the women members of the MWSO went on to find work in other orchestras, helping to prove, as Stark had intended, that women belonged on an equal footing in the classical world.

GRACIELA

Singer
New York, New York, USA
1947

Her full name was Felipa Graciela Pérez y Gutiérrez, but she was known to everyone simply as Graciela, and she was indisputably the First Lady of Afro-Cuban jazz. Born in Havana in 1915, Graciela grew up in a musical family; her foster brother Frank Grillo, (or Francisco Raúl Gutiérrez Grillo or Francisco Perez Gutiérrez, better known as Macho and then professionally as Machito), encouraged her singing and gave her lessons. At sixteen, she started singing professionally with the all-female eleven-piece Orquesta Anacaona, which she did for the next ten years, while also singing, recording, and touring internationally with El Trio Garcia.

In 1943 Machito summoned Graciela to New York to fill in for him as a singer with his band, the Afro-Cubans, because he had been drafted. His musical director was trumpet and sax player Mario Bauzà, a seminal musician and composer.

She was so good—sassy, sultry, superb—that she stayed on even after Machito returned. In the Mambo years, the forties and fifties, the band traveled the world and performed with other jazz greats, including Dizzy Gillespie, Stan Kenton, and Charlie Parker. Graciela, Machito, and Bauzà made music together for thirty-five years until they broke up, principally over a disagreement about the size of the brass section. Graciela continued singing with Bauzà for another twenty years.

When Graciela died in 2010, the musician Bobby Sanabria remarked that "if it wasn't for Gracie you wouldn't have Celia, La Lupe, Gloria Estefan, and J. Lo, Shakira, even Beyoncé, etc., etc. . . . Gracie opened the door for ALL of them." [34]

GUNTA STÖLZL

Textile Artist
Dessau, Germany
1926

The only woman ever promoted to "master" at the Bauhaus, the revolutionary German art and design school, Stölzl poses here with her famous fellow masters on the roof of the building. The Bauhaus was conceived with the promise of a wild new freedom, a fresh adventure after the devastation of World War I. When its founding manifesto included a pledge of equality between the sexes, young women heard the promise and came running: the majority of the first year's students were female.

Yet behind closed doors, Walter Gropius and other school leaders were secretly fretting. They worried that, in view of the perceived inferiority of women, their level of attendance would surely harm the school's reputation. They schemed ways to reduce their participation; one maneuver was to shunt all women into the weaving program. Coincidence? One thinks not: women have been deeply associated with textiles across time and place. The man in charge of the program had himself such contempt for the practice of weaving that he vowed never to weave "a single thread, tie a single knot." [35]

Stölzl was thus assigned to study weaving instead of ceramics, metalworking, architecture, or other disciplines. However, she took to it brilliantly, creating wall hangings, textiles, and carpets of magnetic beauty, colors, and rhythm. Eventually, a group of (female) students pressured the administration to put her in charge of the program and to name her a master along with the legendary men. She soon created a workshop that was successful artistically, technically, and even financially, bringing in much-needed revenue. The all-female workshop fostered close relationships and intense experimentation.

L-R:
JOSEF ALBERS, HINNERK SCHEPER, GEORG MUCHE, LÁSZLÓ MOHOLY-NAGY, HERBERT BAYER, JOOST SCHMIDT, WALTER GROPIUS, MARCEL BREUER, WASSILY KANDINSKY, PAUL KLEE, LYONEL FEININGER, <u>GUNTA STÖLZL</u>, OSKAR SCHLEMMER.

JOVITA IDÁR

Journalist and Activist
Laredo, Texas, USA
1914

Idár was born into it and ran with it. The daughter of a newspaperman and civil rights activist, she went into the family business and then some. At first she tried being a teacher, but after experiencing the hellish conditions faced by poor Mexican-American schoolchildren in South Texas, she turned to activism through journalism. She worked for her father, and when he died in 1914, the year of this photo, she took over.

Here she is at the print shop of *El Progreso* in Laredo, Texas. When she wrote critically about US military intervention in the Mexican Revolution, US Army soldiers and Texas Rangers came to shut down the paper. She cited the First Amendment and stood them down. But her brave defense only delayed the inevitable; the Rangers soon returned and smashed the printing press.

Mexican-American families who had lived there for centuries faced vicious racism from whites in South Texas, who created a version of Jim Crow dubbed "Juan Crow." Signs saying "No Negroes, Mexicans or dogs allowed" were common, as were lynchings.

Idár sometimes wrote under pen names, including Astraea (the Greek goddess of justice) and Ave Negra (Black Bird), to advocate for the causes she believed in: education, workers' rights and unions, women's rights and suffrage, all with a proud love of Mexican culture and language. She was also an organizer, founding and leading organizations for cross-border unity and feminism—a defiant and creative figure who embodies the exceptional genius of some Only Women.

JANE CAMPION

Filmmaker
Cannes, France
2007

I can't imagine people telling me what to do—I just can't imagine it. [36]

—Jane Campion

New Zealand filmmaker Campion won the Cannes Film Festival's highest honor, the Palme d'Or, in 1993 for her film *The Piano*. The festival actually gave the prize as a shared award that year, splitting it between her and Chen Kaige. She was the first-ever woman to win, and she—and many others—fully expected another woman winner would quickly follow. How naive.

Twenty-four years of Onliness later, she protested: "Too long! . . . And before that, there was no one. It's insane . . . . No. No! There's no more guys winning. That's it. It's just going to be women winning from now on." [37]

In 2018 she gained hope, thanks to the global revival of feminist activism. "It's like the Berlin wall coming down, like the end of apartheid. I think we have lived in one of the more ferocious patriarchal periods of our time, the 80s, 90s and noughties. Capitalism is such a macho force. I felt run over." [38] But that year, only four percent of top Hollywood films were directed by women, and not much more in independent cinema. It took three more years until, finally, the 2021 jury awarded the Palme d'Or to Julia Ducournau for her film *Titane*, changing Campion's twenty-eight-year Only status to First overnight.

Pictured here in 2007, Campion was the only woman among thirty-two filmmakers from more than twenty different countries invited by the festival organizers to help celebrate its sixtieth anniversary. A whole world of cinema, with one woman.

First row, L–R: MING-LIANG TSAI, GUS VAN SANT, ROMAN POLANSKI, MANOEL DE OLIVEIRA, AMOS GITAI, ATOM EGOYAN, WALTER SALLES, and ALEJANDRO GONZÁLEZ IÑÁRRITU.

Second row, L–R: ELIA SULEIMAN, THEO ANGELOPOULOS, TAKESHI KITANO, MICHAEL CIMINO, JANE CAMPION, HSIAO-HSIEN HOU, and RAYMOND DEPARDON.

Third row, L–R: BILLE AUGUST, WIM WENDERS, KEN LOACH, ETHAN and JOEL COEN, NANNI MORETTI, and CLAUDE LELOUCH.

Fourth row, L–R: ANDREI KONCHALOVSKY, AKI KAURISMÄKI, KAIGE CHEN, ABBAS KIAROSTAMI, DAVID CRONENBERG, JEAN-PIERRE DARDENNE, LUC DARDENNE, KAR-WAI WONG, OLIVIER ASSAYAS, and RAOUL RUIZ.

NINA SCHULMAN

Filmmaker
Monterey, California, USA
1967

In 1967, the Summer of Love, filmmaker D. A. Pennebaker got $200,000 from ABC to film the rock festival Monterey Pop, and he pulled all his friends onto the crew: Al Maysles, Ricky Leacock, Bob Van Dyke, even the painter Brice Marden—why not?

This illustrious crew, sporting at least five film cameras, which were then nearly exclusively male instruments, included one woman, tucked in the center with a sound recorder over her shoulder: Schulman, a young filmmaker who became the editor of the legendary 1968 documentary that resulted from this shoot. The concert, and the film that immortalized it so well, was the brief and blazing apotheosis of sixties musical heaven. Within just two years of *Monterey Pop's* release, its three greatest stars—Otis Redding, Janis Joplin, and Jimi Hendrix—were all dead. Schulman was a versatile and eclectic talent, moving from

sound to editing to producing. She produced a Nixon-era horror-comedy-satire, 1973's *The Werewolf of Washington*, that was a complete flop at the time. But, in 2020, a director's cut was revived, and film critic Richard Brody praised it as a "scathing sendup." [39]

When Schulman was diagnosed with metastatic breast cancer in 2004, she was disappointed to find no support among what she called the "pink ribbon community," the well-developed support organizations for people with less severe diagnoses. Schulman decided to do something about that, and, the year she was diagnosed, she cofounded the advocacy group Metastatic Breast Cancer Network to provide hope and help to those who were in the same boat she found herself in. The organization has since helped thousands.

MADELINE LINFORD

Newspaper Editor
Manchester, England, UK
1921

To go back to the beginning then, "Miss Linford arrived as a girl in Cross Street in October, 1913, as an assistant in the display advertisement office. She was "lent" to Mr. W. P. Crozier, then news editor, later editor, as a temporary secretary, and stayed in the editorial department where she was the only woman right up to 1944 when Mary Crozier joined the staff. No need, like Dorothy Parker, to put a notice "Men" on her door. They all popped in and out to see her, and she found her isolation among a staff of brilliant men exhilarating and tremendous fun". [40]

So read a profile of Madeline Linford, the first woman editor of England's legendary progressive newspaper *The Guardian*, written fifty years after this photo was taken. Linford was not only the first but, for twenty-five years, the only. A second woman editor was finally hired, who happened to be the daughter of the Editor-in-Chief.

Linford first made a name for herself with her writing and courage when she was sent alone on a mission to postwar Europe. She was then picked "to give birth and nurture" a six-day-a-week page for "the intelligent woman." [41] She much later wrote: "I should hesitate to say that the intelligent was a rarer animal then than she is now: that would be both a betrayal of my contemporaries and, probably, a downright mis-statement. But she was, I think, a more specialised type in an age when culture and higher education were less evenly bestowed upon the sexes." [42]

She seems to have always been very busy. She wrote five novels (the last in 1930) and a biography of the great feminist Mary Wollstonecraft, who remarked that "women have seldom sufficient employment to silence their feelings." [43]

DOROTHY PARKER

Writer
New York, New York, USA
1938

Parker was celebrated in her twenties as The Only Woman in the so-called Vicious Circle, which lunched together for almost a decade at the Algonquin Hotel. Its members were humorists, critics, playwrights, and, most important, creators of the burgeoning world of fashionable magazines, such as *Vanity Fair* and *The New Yorker*—in short, a crowd well placed to publicize Parker's *quips du jour.* Her response to her editor asking for her overdue copy: "Tell him I'm too fucking busy, and vice versa." [44]

She wasn't actually the only woman in the circle—there were others among its twenty-plus informal members— but it is often the case that one woman gets the spotlight and recognition, while the others are framed out. Parker was a founder of the group and is often seen as its Only. A party girl who set the pace, an embodiment of the Roaring Twenties, she was heralded as a new kind of woman: self-supporting, sexually free, bold, fast, funny, with an endless supply of snark—one of the boys but even more fun.

When challenged to use the word horticulture in a sentence, she replied, "You can lead a horticulture, but you can't make her think." [45]

Aside from wit and intelligence, her writing revealed her depression, suicide attempts, failed love, and articulate self-loathing.

Time doth flit; oh shit. [46]

Parker was a lifelong political activist for left causes, and she left her estate to Martin Luther King Jr.

Seated, L–R: FRITZ FOORD, WOLCOTT GIBBS, FRANK CASE and <u>DOROTHY PARKER</u>.

Standing, L–R: ALAN CAMPBELL (Parker's husband), ST. CLAIR MCKELWAY, RUSSELL MALONEY, and JAMES THURBER.

LISETTE DAMMAS

Juror
New York, New York, USA
1951

Dammas, the only woman juror in the American Cold War spy trial of Julius and Ethel Rosenberg, was a fifty-year-old married mother from the Bronx. She, like all her fellow jury members, quickly convicted the mild-mannered couple of giving dangerous information to the Soviet Union. The jury knew that a likely punishment was execution.

New York allowed women onto juries in 1927, but their presence wasn't required. Although winning jury rights took years after voting rights, New York State was still relatively progressive; Mississippi did not *allow* women jurors until 1968. The rules in the Rosenberg case barred juror candidates who knew anything at all about the case, which had been a tabloid sensation. Also barred was anyone who objected to the death penalty, so the end result was a bloodthirsty bunch who'd been living under rocks. Specifically, no Jews and only one woman.

The defense attorneys were pleased to have a mother on the jury, as they hoped she would be sympathetic to Ethel,

who had two small sons. But Ethel showed no emotion in the trial and was seen as a kind of witch. She was essentially burned as one too; the press gleefully described her botched electrocution, which required more than one torturous attempt before succeeding.

After the trial, supporters of the Rosenbergs hoped that the lack of Jewish jurors could form the basis of an appeal; however, none argued that Ethel's right to a jury of her peers was violated by the dearth of women. Recently released files show that Ethel was innocent, convicted on the basis of false testimony by her brother and his wife. Her husband, Julius, was indeed guilty—though the spy material he passed along was not damaging, as he believed it to be.

After Dammas's death, a reporter asked her daughter if her mother had ever wavered in her opinion about the Rosenbergs' guilt. She said, "My mother never wavered in her opinion in her life." [47]

FRANCES PERKINS

Politician
Washington, D.C., USA
c. 1939

Feminism means revolution and I am a revolutionist. [48]
—Frances Perkins

Perkins is a monumental First and Great Exception. The first woman member of an American presidential cabinet, she was Franklin D. Roosevelt's secretary of labor for his entire time in office, from 1933 to 1945. Often called the architect of the New Deal, she outlawed child labor and was responsible for the creation of Social Security, unemployment insurance, the forty-hour work week, minimum wage, maximum work hours, and myriad other worker protections and social support measures.

After studying economics and sociology, working as a teacher, and volunteering as a social worker, she began working to protect urban factory workers, including women and children. She successfully lobbied to legally limit their work hours in New York State to fifty-four per week. Her career really began with the infamous Triangle Shirtwaist factory fire in New York in 1911, which she actu-ally witnessed. The 146 gruesome and unnecessary deaths of trapped workers, mostly women and children, pushed the city to create a Committee on Safety, and Perkins was appointed to head it.

She married and later had two successive relationships with women. She was prescient, knowing that she was a First who may not soon find a second or third and wrote, "The door might not be opened to a woman again for a long, long time, and I had a kind of duty to other women to walk in and sit down on the chair that was offered, and so establish the right of others long hence and far distant in geography to sit in the high seats." [49] The second appointment of a woman to a presidential cabinet indeed came twenty years after Perkins was sworn in. The third came twenty years after that.

KATHERINE HOWARD

Politician
Chicago, Illinois, USA
1952

As secretary of the Republican National Committee, Howard won the honor of speaking at the podium of the 1952 Republican Convention. Behind her, seemingly oblivious to her presence, a gaggle of state governors and party officials continue their confab.

Howard had worked her way up in Republican circles for years, and she went on to a number of high-powered positions. But that moment at the podium made everyone know her name—not because of her words, but her feet. The television techs would not adjust the microphone for her height, and she thought nobody would see if she slipped off her heels to be better positioned to be heard. She never imagined that there would be TV cameras behind her, which lingered on her stocking feet as she spoke. She ended up titling her 1977 memoir *With My Shoes Off.*

After the convention nominated Eisenhower as the Republican Party's candidate, Howard was hired to join his national election campaign for president. When she had her job interview with an official, she said: "He I guess looked me over, and took me on as the woman member of the campaign policy committee," she recalled. The woman member: a description that succinctly underscores the job of many Only Women.

The idea of tokenism has acquired different shadings of meanings over time. Today in the United States, the term *tokenism* is usually used to describe a false gesture made by those in power to include a single representative of a group in response to a perceived need to *appear* inclusive. Nominally a gesture of appeasement, while silently it insults, the practice of tokenism has a PR motive: it's "window-dressing," done for show.

The Republican presidential campaign in 1952 was pre-tokenism in that sense: those guys weren't worried about PR or being attacked if they didn't hire a woman. Rather they wanted a female member because they thought she would help them: they actually believed that a lone woman could tell them how to appeal to women, while also keeping the candidate's wife company on the campaign trail.

Tokenism can also describe that older, weirder, kind of magical thinking, in which a One can symbolically stand in for all or many, adding power way beyond her Onliness by virtue of her ability to represent her apparently essentially identical sisters. In that sense, Howard was a token for sure.

KOMAKO KIMURA

Performing Artist
New York, New York, USA
1917

In the beginning, woman was truly the sun. An authentic person. Now she is the moon, a wan and sickly moon, dependent on another, reflecting another's brilliance. [50]

—Raichō Hiratsuku, feminist contemporary of Komako Kimura

Kimura said she was fighting to win Japanese women their place in the sun. She is pictured here on Fifth Avenue in New York, just as the American movement for women's suffrage was flexing its hard-earned muscle in yet another march. This time the feeling was triumphant—it took three hours for the march to pass by, from head to tail—and ten days later came a big victory when the men in state government finally voted to let women vote in New York elections.

Even though she was surrounded by tens of thousands of women, Kimura poses here against a backdrop of curious male onlookers. That may have been the press photographer's idea, of course, but Kimura was an accomplished dramatic artist who knew how to make an appearance and stand out from the crowd.

Early hardship pushed her toward creating her stand-out persona: she began performing in Japan at a very young age to support her family. As a young woman, she cofounded a Japanese women's movement called the New True Woman, and its magazine, which criticized marriage, discussed birth control, and tied feminism to other dimensions of a just world.

In 1908 she had a baby before she married the father, incurring heavy disapprobation. Barred from giving public lectures, she responded by writing a one-woman play she titled *Ignorance* – a not subtle criticism of her censorship

by the state. When the Japanese government tried to shut it down, she made all the tickets free. She was arrested and represented herself at her trial, winning a broad audience for her feminist arguments.

Kimura came to the United States in 1917 to study American feminism hoping to counter the discouragement she had felt at home. She stayed for several years, meeting the president, the first congresswoman, and other luminaries while supporting herself by giving dance performances and teaching acupuncture and other skills.

In an interview soon after her arrival, she credited her unusual personal independence and perspective to her background in the theater. "Few careers are open to women in Japan," she said. "The stage more than any other career, however, offers to [a] woman a chance to acquaint herself with the times and their character." [51] The theater gave her a rare freedom and an entrée into the all-male world of public concerns.

Japanese women won the right to vote in 1946, when women's equal rights before the law were written into Japan's new constitution. That constitution was drafted by a group of twenty-five Americans under the occupation authority; the clause for women's rights was written by Beate Sirota Gordon, a twenty-two year old who was the committee's only woman.

GERTRUDE BELL

Imperialist
Cairo, Egypt
1921

The only woman here, under her big-brimmed hat, was a perennial Only Woman. Bell spent much of her life in all-male spaces: reading history at the University of Oxford, mountaineering in the Alps, crisscrossing the Middle East, founding an archaeological museum, and serving as an officer in the occupying British government. The daughter of a very rich man, Bell grew up with all the attitudes of her class but, after having not married by the age of thirty, she threw herself first into adventure, languages, and travel, and then into politics and power.

Her first trip to the Middle East was a visit to her uncle, the British ambassador in Tehran, and she liked it. She became fluent in Arabic, Persian, and Turkish, and made extended expeditions to Egypt, Saudi Arabia, Syria, Iran, and Iraq, traveling with gifts and retinues of guides and servants, learning who was who in each country. She wrote books, a monumental report on the politics of the region, and about 1,600 letters describing her experiences, and she took thousands of photographs. In 1926, at fifty-eight, she died of an overdose of sleeping pills in Baghdad.

The subject of more than ten flattering biographies, a film starring Nicole Kidman, and a documentary with Tilda Swinton voicing her letters, she is nevertheless often described as "forgotten" or "written out of history." She has been called "Queen of the Desert," "the female Lawrence of Arabia," "the female Indiana Jones," "Lady of Iraq," "Imperial Feminist," and "Queen of Quagmire." The writer Rory Stewart claims that her biographers "have generally ignored her intriguing combination of creativity, honesty, intelligence, and wrongheaded idiocy in favor of celebrating her as a female genius." [52]

In this photo of the 1921 Cairo Conference, she is posing with Winston Churchill, T. E. Lawrence (he of Arabia), and other luminaries. In the lower left the only Black man present sits on the floor with two lion cubs that had come from Somaliland and were in transit to the London Zoo. The conference concerned the fate of the then Ottoman provinces of Baghdad, Basra, and Mosul, which the British had occupied during World War I. In 1920 they decided to make a country out of them. Bell was involved in that fateful decision, and she helped import a new client king and royal family for the created country of Iraq. In spite of her actions, her letters express some critical understanding: "We have made an immense failure here." [53]

What she learned from all that living in a man's world was apparently not flattering to women: she was against women's suffrage, even heading up an organization to campaign against it.

AMY GERALDINE "DINAH" STOCK

Anti-Imperialist
Manchester, England, UK
c. 1945

Stock and her hat here are both rather smiley as she seems to be playing the role of a hostess to these distinguished and serious besuited men. It was a crucial moment, right after the war, when former British colonies around the world were pushing for radical change and this was a joint meeting of the West African Students' Union and the West African National Secretariat, a Pan-Africanist movement founded by Kwame Nkrumah, the future leader of Ghana (seated far right front).

A.G. Stock, known to most as Dinah, was a lifelong committed anti-colonialist. As an undergraduate at Oxford University, Stock was said to be the only white student who often attended the Majlis, a society founded by South Asian students who gathered to debate issues, including independence from the British empire. At twenty-five, she became secretary of the Centre Against Imperialism.

A few years later, she befriended the young student who came to be known as Jomo Kenyatta, the future first president of newly liberated Kenya. She edited his book, and in 1937 he moved in with her. She supported him in innumerable ways, getting his articles published, hosting visitors, and finding them a safe spot in the English countryside, where they spent the war years together. Some have denied that theirs was a romantic relationship, but she wrote that she was the single person who knew him best in the world. She was his intellectual equal yet served as his helpmeet; she believed in him and his cause and put her energies in his service, working a day job as a secretary to support him. Many of their activities were well documented by the hard-working spies of the English secret service, who kept them under surveillance for years.

Kenyatta returned to Africa after the war, and she took up teaching positions around the world, from Jaipur to Uganda. At the University in Dhaka, she fell in love with the Bengali culture, language, and landscape. Stock, who never married and remained childfree, returned for two years after their revolution and wrote a well-regarded memoir that was rescued from oblivion, thanks to a 2017 edition.

First row, L–R: I. T. A. WALLACE-JOHNSON (second from left), AMY GERALDINE "DINAH" STOCK (center), BANKOLE AWOONER-RENNER (second from right), and KWAME NKRUMAH (far right).

LATIFE HANIM

Wife
Turkey
1923

If "power is an aphrodisiac," as Henry Kissinger perhaps wishfully remarked, it might explain why the marriage between Kemal Atatürk, the founding father of the Republic of Turkey, and Latife Hanım, lasted even the brief two years it did.

Latife, seated here with her new husband and his officers after their wedding, was born into a well-educated, wealthy family, in Smyrna (now Izmir, Turkey) in 1898. She had studied law at the Sorbonne and was in London learning English (one of her seven languages) when the man who would become her husband was waging the Turkish War of Independence—and living with a woman he called his assistant.

They met in 1922, when Turkish troops marched toward Smyrna to find a headquarters, and Latife and her family opened their homes. But she was not quite so open to his advances: when Atatürk tried to kiss her, she fired a gun into the air three times, vowing to kill herself on a fourth attempt because he was necessary for the country, but she was not.

Ignoring the red flag, the confirmed bachelor, seventeen years her senior, proposed marriage. Who could have been more irresistible to the architect of Turkish independence than the living embodiment of his ideal—the "modern Turkish woman," who could write his speeches, suggest new laws for women's rights—while elevating him to a higher social class? And who could be more irresistible to a feistily independent woman, than a bad-boy freedom fighter with a devastating effect on the opposite sex? [54]

However Latife had little patience for Atatürk's drinking habits and late-night soirees. According to existing accounts, she would retire and then bang on the floorboards to let her husband know it was time for bed.

At one reception, she refused to play the piano for the guests, so Atatürk asked her cousin to play instead. Afterward, Latife berated her husband. "He played incorrectly," she said. "Why did you let him continue?" Then she furiously slapped her fan in her palm, cutting herself. When her husband tried to slap her, she smeared her blood on his face.

It was the slap heard round the world. [55]

Ambassadors sent encrypted messages that said, "Atatürk's wife slapped him in front of commanders," "The Turkish Republic's founder lost face," and "A coup may break out any time." [56] It was difficult for Atatürk to end his marriage, but he could not tolerate such humiliation. Latife Hanım was escorted back to her father's home, where she maintained a decidedly uncharacteristic silence for the rest of her life.

ANNA HELLER ROZENTAL

Bundist
Vienna, Austria
1931

Rozental devoted her life—until her death in prison—to organizing and helping Jewish workers, who faced terrible working conditions, as well as routine anti-Semitic violence. She grew up in Lithuania when it was part of the Russian Empire, in a wealthy family that then fell on hard times. She became a dentist, which was not uncommon for women at the time (the majority of Lithuania's dentists were Jewish and female) and married a doctor. The city of Vilna, as Vilnius was called by its Jewish inhabitants, was a dynamic cultural crossroads, full of political and intellectual ferment. Drawn to Marxism and early Zionism, Rozental and her husband became involved with underground efforts, called jargon committees, to print and distribute political literature in Yiddish to Jewish workers.

In 1897 Rozental was one of thirteen young activists and workers who met secretly for three days in an attic, to found the General Union of Jewish Workers or the Bund (which means union in Yiddish). The Bund was to become a storied organization that blossomed in many locations across Eastern Europe and as far as the United States in the decades to come. It was the first Jewish political party, formed to promote socialism, workers' rights, education, and Yiddish culture. The members were antireligious and anti-Zionist, citing the principle of *doykeyt* (hereness) and the idea that "wherever we live is our home." [57] Women

played a significant role, since the party recognized they were important participants in class struggle: many worked in small manufacturers, making everything from cigarettes to stockings and envelopes.

Rozental and her husband were arrested in 1902 and sent to Siberia, where they were held until they were released due to the 1905 Russian Revolution. Rozental got right back to work; her commitment to the Bund never flagged.

She is seen here as a member of the Bund's delegation to the 1931 Socialist International. Describing the congress as a fitting jewel for Vienna, "the showcase of European socialism," the *New York Times* gushed that the gathering attracted representatives from thirty-four Socialist parties as well as members of organizations for socialist women, socialist students, socialist nature lovers, socialist temperance, and seventy thousand worker-athletes who came to compete in their own socialist Olympics! [58]

Rozental was eventually arrested again, this time by the Soviets, and died in a prison camp sometime in the early years of World War II. Her intersectional vision of an ethnic *and* class liberation, of freeing people from anti-Semitism *and* capitalism, was almost extinguished, with millions of Jewish lives.

SOPHIE MOSSEAU

Unknown
Fort Laramie, Wyoming, USA
c. 1868–70

The people in this group portrait all look a little like chess pieces on an odd board, each facing in its own direction and perhaps afforded its own style of locomotion. Three almost matching pairs that might slide, hop, or zoom, and one unlike the others—the only one whose gaze catches the camera's. Is she queen or pawn? She seems at once like the most and least important figure: she is the small, calm, central person, and yet she is literally being overlooked by the two powerful men looking at each other.

The photographer noted the names of the six white men in their clothing that announces their positions of power, but not the name of the girl wrapped in her blanket. The men were members of the US government's Peace Commission, formed in 1867 by the Congress to negotiate treaties on behalf of the US government, with several tribes.

The members of the commission, which most historians agree was a failed initiative, included: a civilian (third from the right), a US Army colonel, and four generals, including William Tecumseh Sherman, he of the infamous Sherman's March that laid waste to the South at the close of the Civil War just thirteen years before. It is Sherman in his cape to the left of the girl, facing over her head the civilian member, a liberal from Boston.

Somebody else, not the photographer, contributed the information that the girl was Sophie Mosseau, daughter of a Lakota Sioux mother and a French Canadian trapper father.

We don't know why she was posing in such a memorable configuration with these gentlemen.

L–R: GENERAL ALFRED HOWE TERRY, GENERAL WILLIAM S. HARNEY, GENERAL WILLIAM TECUMSEH SHERMAN, SOPHIE MOSSEAU, JOHN B. SANBORN, COLONEL SAMUEL F. TAPPAN, and GENERAL CHRISTOPHER C. AUGER.

SATSUKI KATAYAMA

Politician
Tokyo, Japan
2018

Appointed as Minister of Regional Revitalization and Gender Equity when Prime Minister Shinzo Abe reshuffled his twenty-member cabinet in late 2018, Katayama was the only woman remaining. Abe acknowledged that "the ratio of women in the cabinet is low" but said Katayama "has enough presence for two or even three people." [59] The 2020 cabinet had two women members. Abe was well known for his oft-repeated empty promises to bring more women into government and to push for a society in which "women shine." The government had even used the slogan "Just one woman is not enough." [60]

This photo shows the official declaration ceremony that introduces the new government in Tokyo's Imperial Palace. It was well publicized that right before this photo was taken, a cabinet official told Katayama that her proposed outfits (she brought two) were unacceptable. They were not of one solid color, and they were not long enough. He suggested that silver would be a good choice of color. She ran out and, miraculously, got back in time with the perfect shiny silver dress.

UNKNOWN

Mascot
Annapolis, Maryland, USA
1894

Identified on the negative of this image held by the Library of Congress only as "Mascot," the young woman placed in the center of this graduating class at the US Naval Academy, staring straight at the camera with a grim expression and a fabulous hat, looks like a lady with her gorgeous outfit. But there's no clue who she was. A daughter of the Superintendent or another officer? A little sister? She is not even a token: she was not admitted with the others—the US Naval Academy didn't admit women until 1976. She is an *other*, placed at the heart, in a position of honor and presumably affection.

A *mascotte* was originally a good luck charm, a rare French dialect word. It was popularized first in France and then internationally via a hit play, *La Mascotte* (1880), a French comic operetta in which the title character was a young woman whose presence brought extraordinary good luck. The hitch: her magic depended on her

virginity. Hijinks and comedy ensue, as various nefarious Frenchmen work to thwart the inclinations of their nature. In the United States, the play created a kind of craze for the word—it turned up everywhere: the name of a New Orleans newspaper, the brand of a "patent medicine for curing Gonorrhea and Gleet," a racehorse. Only the year before this photograph was taken, the Navy football team introduced its first official mascot, a figure who survives today, Bill the Goat.

Many of the images in this book show the phenomenon of mascotism without naming it so conveniently. A woman who serves as a good luck charm for the group of men is a configuration that predates tokenism. Somehow it was pleasing to the men, and it may well have been flattering and fun for many of the women. Though possibly not this one: she doesn't look thrilled.

021339. GRADUATING CLASS 1894. U.S. NAVAL ACADEMY.   DETROIT PHOTOGRAPHIC CO.

CHRISTINA BROOM

Photographer
Oxford, England, UK
1938

Mrs. Albert Broom, as Christina Broom was known, is posing here with the Oxford University boat race crew, holding a doll that was the team's mascot. The doll helps underline her own tiny size and contrasting old age, as well as how fully at ease everyone looks. She knew both the photographer and her fellow subjects exceedingly well, and they have placed her in a position of honor and affection.

Broom was a pioneering photographer—the first woman press photographer of England—and this photo near the end of her life was taken by her daughter, Winifred Margaret Broom. Christina first picked up a camera at the age of forty, in need of making a living, and Winifred left school to serve as her assistant and partner. The Oxford and Cambridge boat crews were some of Christina's earliest clients, and she covered them formally and informally for thirty years—they were called "Mrs. Broom's boys."

Broom was legendarily indefatigable, pulling all-nighter printing sessions and getting herself to locations via wheelbarrow when she was unwell. She left behind forty thousand photographs, with subjects ranging widely, from royalty to buildings. Her most acclaimed pictures are her extraordinary coverage of two fighting forces in the United Kingdom: the soldiers of World War I and the suffragists who were tirelessly protesting and organizing for women's rights.

Shipyard Worker
Aberdeen, Washington, USA
1918

Against the backdrop of World War I, this group was in a national spotlight, as participants in an audacious and much-publicized challenge to build a "Wonder Ship" for the war effort in record time. In seventeen *days*, to be exact.

The metalworkers here were among the 1,200 men and women who worked around the clock to speed the construction of the wooden steamship at Grays Harbor shipyard, strategically located near the lumber-producing forests on the Pacific coast. Their efforts transfixed the nation day after day, and when they successfully launched the SS *Aberdeen* on the seventeenth day, the town and nation rejoiced. Two weeks later there was even greater rejoicing, when the armistice finally put an end to the war, leaving the SS *Aberdeen* redundant after all.

The only woman here strikes a triumphant pose right in the middle and seems full of beans and fun. Is she just "one of the guys," another metalworker? It is certainly possible: photographs of the shipyard's other work crews—the joiners, for example—do include a few handfuls of women; in wartime it's common for new jobs to open to women due to shortages of male labor. But her attitude, her literal elevation, and her Onliness suggest that her role is likely different than the men's. Perhaps she is a friendly visitor, a figure of encouragement and fun, in a version of the mascotism that characterizes some other Only Women.

Girard

Metal Workers
S.S. Aberdeen

EMMELINE PANKHURST

Suffragette
London, England, UK
1914

On May 21, 1914, fifty-five-year-old Pankhurst, a militant activist out of prison on parole, led two hundred women to Buckingham Palace to deliver a petition to King George V demanding women's suffrage. They were met by a crowd of onlookers, press photographers, and two thousand policemen. When stopped at the gates, marchers attacked police with batons and vice versa. The police charged, numerous petitioners were injured, and sixty-seven suffragettes were arrested—including Pankhurst, in the moment—pictured here.

Pankhurst, founder and leader of the Women's Social and Political Union (WSPU), had a great gift for using the media to transmit her message, generating publicity and photo ops that drew eyeballs to the mass circulation newspapers emerging from Fleet Street. Witness the masterstroke of this particular photograph: Pankhurst, weakened by hunger strikes and in distress, being carried against her will from the scene by Superintendent Francis Harry Rolfe. This tiny, apparently defenseless female being manhandled in the name of state power was, in fact, a wily and implacable opponent who spent forty years organizing and mobilizing an army of thousands of angry disenfranchised women across the country.

When Britain declared war on Germany, just two and a half months after Pankhurst's arrest, the WSPU suspended its campaign and its members' acts of violence—smashing windows, planting explosives, arson (this last largely orchestrated by Pankhurst's daughter Christabel)—to support the country in the war effort. As World War I ground on, Pankhurst seized the opportunity to work on a new front in the struggle for women's rights, both at home and internationally: moving women into the industrial labor force, to fill the paid jobs vacated by men fighting abroad.

She died in 1928, just months before Britain passed the Equal Franchise Act, which gave women equal rights to vote. Two years after that, her statue was erected in Westminster to honor her tireless efforts and those of the rest of her family.

KATHRINE SWITZER

Athlete
Boston, Massachusetts, USA
1967

The Boston Marathon was all male for seventy years. Its founder was inspired by the first modern Olympic Games in 1896 and seems to have shared the view of Baron Pierre de Coubertin, the founder of the modern Olympics, that participation by women athletes would be "impractical, uninteresting, unaesthetic, and, I do not hesitate to add, incorrect." [61]

Switzer, a college student with a devoted running coach, sent in her three dollar registration fee, signed her name K. V. Switzer instead of Kathrine, and got an official number. She was the only woman among the 741 runners that day—unbeknownst to the race officials. But one got wise at mile four (kilometer six). "I jerked my head around quickly and looked square into the most vicious face I'd ever seen. A big man, a huge man, with bared teeth was set to pounce, and before I could react he grabbed my shoulder and flung me back, screaming, 'Get the hell out of my race and give me those numbers!' Then he swiped down my front, trying to rip off my bib number, just as I leapt backward from him. He missed the numbers, but I was so surprised and frightened that I slightly wet my pants and turned to run." [62]

When Jock Semple, the race official, tried to grab Switzer, her boyfriend's body blocked him. "There was a thud—whoomph!—and Jock was airborne. He landed on the roadside like a pile of wrinkled clothes. Now I felt terror. We've killed this guy Jock." [63]

Nevertheless, she persisted. As she kept running, her fear turned to anger, then elation, and finally to determination. "About 20 miles into the race, I came to the conclusion that when I finished, I was going to try to be a better athlete and try to create opportunities for women so they would experience the same sense of power, strength and freedom that I had. When I crossed the finish line, it wasn't like 'Wow! I did it—I did my first marathon.' It was like 'Wow! I've got a life plan!'" [64]

Switzer went on to become a legend in women's sports. She has now run over forty marathons and has devoted her career to encouraging female runners, including a successful campaign to create the Olympic women's marathon. She believes that the attack and the photo helped galvanize public opinion.

When she returned to Boston to run in 2017, she was seventy and just one of 13,700 women, almost half of all contestants.

LUCY KOMISAR

Activist and Journalist
New York, New York, USA
1970

McSorley's Old Ale House in Manhattan's East Village has long claimed the title of oldest Irish pub in New York. In 1923 the poet E. E. Cummings wrote a poem that begins: "i was sitting in mcsorley's. outside it was New York and beautifully snowing. Inside snug and evil." [65]

And yet of all its high profile patrons, there was nary a dame among them. The place had never allowed women through the door, a feature that only increased its appeal to every young and visiting fellow, seeking the frisson offered by this legendary masculine sanctum.

The sex segregation was not unusual in the sixties and seventies. Many American establishments refused entry to women, from the fancy and storied Russian Tea Room and Oak Room at the Plaza hotel in New York, to dive bars on every corner, some at all hours; others only at lunch. Some required women to use a special entrance. In the sixties

"women could find selected places to go for a drink in some parts of the United States, but the majority of bars remained closed to them." [66]

Komisar was vice president of the National Organization for Women when, on August 11, 1970, she went to McSorley's to mark the day when sex discrimination in public places was banned. In this photo, she is the Only Woman as space invader, an alien from a more fabulous planet. The *New York Times* front page chronicled Komisar's experience and what she was wearing—purple jumpsuit, sunglasses, sandals! She experienced, shall we say, friction, at the door, and in the moments after this one pictured, when she got her mug of ale from the bar, she ended up wearing another, thanks to the young men behind her.

By 1973 very few American public spaces remained *legally* male only.

SHIRLEY CHISHOLM

Politician
New York, New York, USA
1972

Chisholm appears here on the political television show *Meet the Press*, with the other Democratic candidates for US president in 1972. She is a "Multiple First": first African American woman elected to Congress, first Black person to run for a major party's nomination, and first woman ever to seek the Democratic nomination. But she herself was not impressed: "That I am a national figure because I was the first person in 192 years to be at once a congressman, black, and a woman proves, I would think, that our society is not yet either just or free." [67]

First is a designation that is as complicated as Only. Being a First is a well-worn honorific, a badge of achievement in a society that is striving to dismantle multiple hierarchies and exclusions. But the stories of many of the women in this book demand a reappraisal of the meaning of being a First, just as it does for being an Only. Firsts are *everywhere*, because every little social barrier becomes its own story, its own milestone. Even when there are historical waves of women entering public life (during wartime, for example), gender integration often occurs piecemeal: each arena has its own separate history of women struggling to enter and progress, inch by inch, job by job. Shola Lynch, the director of a documentary on Chisholm, says we must be cautious, even suspicious, of the simple term *first*. She argues that its use flattens and, paradoxically, tends to devalue the very person we want to honor. "Relegating Chisholm to a 'first' positions her as immortal, thereby erasing the effort and guts it took to act out on her principles. It also takes her out of context of historical struggles and activism." [68] The term implies victory, while Lynch's film brings home the disappointments and betrayals Chisholm endured.

The persistence of patriarchy was a key theme for Chisholm. "Men are men," she said. "When I ran for the Congress, when I ran for president, I met more discrimination as a woman than for being black." She called for women to "become revolutionaries" and declared that "we must replace the old, negative thoughts about our femininity with positive thoughts and positive action affirming it, and more." But she also warned of the cost: "We must prepare ourselves educationally, economically, and psychologically in order that we will be able to accept and bear with the sanctions that society will immediately impose upon us. . . . This is hard, and especially hard for women, who are taught not to rebel from infancy, from the time they are first wrapped in pink blankets, the color of their caste." [69]

First row, L–R: HENRY JACKSON and SHIRLEY CHISHOLM.

Second row, L–R: GEORGE MCGOVERN, HUBERT HUMPHREY, and EDMUND MUSKIE.

MING SMITH

Photographer
New York, New York, USA
1973

When the photographer Smith was invited in 1972 to join the Kamoinge Workshop collective, a group of Black photographers formed in 1963, she became the youngest member and the first woman. She talks about her young self as "shy, very very quiet. . . . I hardly spoke then," and she credits the collective with taking her under its wing and giving her a place to grow as an artist. [70]

As Smith explains, Kamoinge, which means "a group of people acting together" in the Kikuyu language of Kenya, "came out of the Black Power movement. . . . We spent a lot of time looking at images and critiquing, trying to change them, and to have another point of view from what the media was showing us . . . then, there weren't that many images of us, and they were mostly negative images. They didn't show the love and humanity of our people." Smith says she "never saw images of our great culture anywhere, anywhere." [71]

Smith remained the only woman member for twenty years but is not very interested in that. In 2019 she said, "Someone asked me once, 'Well, how does it feel to be the first woman in Kamoinge?' And I said, without thinking about it, I didn't even realize I was a woman. I mean that didn't ever come—until the last five years I never even really thought about it." [72]

She is often cited as the first Black woman to have her photographs acquired by New York's Museum of Modern Art, a lofty cultural imprimatur that did not have the impact that many may imagine: the acquisition fee didn't even cover the cost of printing the two prints they acquired, and, as she says, "for forty years, there was nothing, no shows, no artist talks." Later she said it was as if she'd won an Academy Award and nobody knew about it. [73]

She married a jazz musician, had a son named Mingus, and, luckily for the world, continued to take photographs. She is known for a surrealist sensibility with an ethereal, fugitive quality—figures half seen and dissolving. She uses double exposures and painting on prints, among other interventions, working in dark places with only natural light and perfecting the blur.

Her work includes many portraits of African American artists, from Grace Jones to Sun Ra and Tina Turner; conceptual portfolios; self-portraits; and street photography from around the world. "Street photography is walking around and making something out of nothing, making art from something that you see every day," she says. "Making something out of nothing. I think that's like jazz." [74]

VALENTINA TERESHKOVA

Cosmonaut
Former USSR
1963

This image of the first six Russian cosmonauts is remarkable for the fact that three of them seem to be watching a bug crawling across the floor. Even more remarkable is that one of the assembled is a woman: twenty-six-year-old Tereshkova was a parachute-jumping enthusiast and avid Communist—two attributes that helped ensure her selection—when she flew solo on the Vostok 6 in 1963, spending almost three days in space, orbiting the Earth forty-eight times. After reentering Earth's atmosphere, she parachuted out about four miles (six kilometers) above the surface. Awarded the title Hero of the USSR, she is the youngest woman ever to have gone into space and the only woman to fly solo, piloting her own craft with manual controls.

Back on solid ground, Tereshkova continued her education, earning a doctorate in engineering, and played nice with the party, joining the elite and becoming a politician who served as a member of the Supreme Soviet as well as the Presidium of the Supreme Soviet and the Central Committee of the Communist Party. She was valuable to the state as a mascot, a civic ambassador, and a public diplomat who made appearances domestically and, in the first seven years after her flight into space, forty-two trips abroad.

For her seventieth birthday in 2007, she visited President Putin, whom she has described as "a splendid person." In 2011 she was elected to the Duma, Russia's legislative body, and in 2020 she proposed a constitutional amendment that would allow Putin to run for two more terms as president.

It's remarkable how often the first of something can remain the First and Only for a long time. It was nineteen years before the Soviets sent the second woman to space and a nice round twenty years before Sally Ride became the first American woman in 1983.

Tereshkova always regretted not having the chance to return to space. In 2007 she volunteered to go to Mars with a special offer: "I am ready to go without flying back." [75]

BETSY WADE

Newspaper Editor
New York, New York, USA
1975

When Wade got the job as a copy editor at the *New York Times* in 1956, after a year of interviews, she became the first woman copy editor on the news desk in over a century. Four years before, she had been fired from her previous job, at the *New York Herald Tribune*, for being pregnant. Here she imagined that maybe her desk would be set up behind some kind of screen, such was her awareness of being an intruding female animal. She dressed in the most conservative clothes she could, hoping to be able to "sit in the middle of an ocean of men and not be noticed." [76] Thus armored up, she got to work.

Against her wishes, the bosses did try the inevitable and moved her to the "woman's page"—for those too young to remember, a long-standing and so-labeled section in every American newspaper where one found items perceived to be of interest to women: fashion, food, and gossip. She got out of there and back to the news desk as soon as she could, and there she reigned, as pictured here, for decades, stringing behind her a lengthening list of firsts as she moved up editorial ladders. She had an illustrious career at the newspaper, forty-five years in all, editing the Pentagon Papers and numerous other journalistic touchstones.

The *Times* hung on to the outdated Mrs. and Miss titles for an embarrassingly long time, despite the efforts of women on the paper; finally, in 1986, under Wade's pencil, the new usage of Ms. was deemed fit to print.

Some of her most important work was not editing but organizing, agitating, and suing. She was deeply involved in the Newspaper Guild union and teaching journalism. And in 1974 she spearheaded one of the biggest and earliest major employment discrimination lawsuits on behalf of the five hundred female employees of the *Times*. After four years, the case was settled, with both sides claiming victory. She extracted concrete hiring changes at all levels of the paper and compensation for "delayed career advancement or denied opportunity."

Secretary
London, England, UK
1964

The twenty white men who have a seat at the table here are the members of an august body, the National Economic Development Council, created to bring UK government, labor, and industry representatives together. In the twenty-five years of the council's existence, it never had a female member. The only woman at the 1964 meeting pictured here does not have a seat at the table; she is seated *behind* the men seated at the table, which means that she is playing a supporting role, as secretary or perhaps another kind of aide.

Some Only Women enter the male sphere *in spite* of being a woman, while others are there *because* they are women. A woman's job, in other words, can provide a kind of pass into all-male spaces. An executive secretary, for example, was always female and often swam in a sea of suits. She was there, of course, as a certified Other—and a subordinate at that. Meanwhile, a lower-status secretary got no such entrée, but belonged with many other women in the typing pool, or in a row of women's desks outside the office doors of male managers. The status of the secretary is deeply involved with gender. The word itself is related to *secret*—implying a discreet and thus potentially impor-

tant assistant—and the position was always male until the advent of the modern office, with its paperwork and newfangled machines. The entry of women into the office was slow and contested, but by 1920 the secretary was well established and female.

The term "pink collar" was popularized in 1977, when Louise Kapp Howe used it to argue that after decades in the labor market, the masses of women were still concentrated in a few particularly low-paying jobs. Secretary was the most common job for American women in 1950—and still is today by most counts (although now it's called administrative assistant or its variants). The other most common jobs for women are also mostly unchanged: retail workers and cashiers; teachers and caregivers for children; nurses and health-care assistants; and cleaners. While there is a lot of focus on the *glass ceiling*—another 1970s coinage that describes the invisible barriers to career achievement—a slightly more recent metaphor deserves more attention: the *sticky floor*, which refers to the various ways that the great majority of women, especially women of color, are disproportionately stuck in low-wage jobs that keep them in poverty.

Biochemist
Denver, Colorado, USA
1946

Model
Paris, France
c. 1900

The American Society of Sugar Beet Technologists (ASSBT) works to make extracting sugar from the lowly beetroot an efficient, sustainable, and profitable process. Here, at their 1946 assembly, their numbers included exactly one woman: a memorably crisp, even chic-looking person if you can pick her out among the men.

The ASSBT is now led by distinguished plant scientist Anna Murphy, and in 2021, twenty percent of the membership was female. Murphy and her staff undertook to identify the woman, but seventy-five years had erased all trace. Finally, fine print in an old catalog revealed that she was, in fact, a future giant of science.

Roboz was a Hungarian who had already faced threats as a Jew and barriers as a woman. To escape anti-semitic educational quotas she earned her PhD in Vienna, and then, in 1940, fled to the United States.

She landed a job studying the potato and then moved to aloe vera at CalTech—which barred women from professorships. So she moved again, to the University of Wyoming, where she studied—sugar beets! Thereafter, she migrated into biochemistry and helped create the field of neurochemistry, making discoveries about the nervous system and a substance called myelin and its role in multiple sclerosis. She published widely, including one book about brain proteins and another about her husband Hans Einstein, son of Albert.

What is she doing among all these men? She looks relaxed, with her hand on a friendly steadying shoulder as she stands on something to take her mock-serious part in the game, gazing soberly at the full frontal nudity of the lively "corpse." Even if she leaps out as the only woman, she seems to be a fringe player.

The men are artists—perhaps some students or teachers—affiliated with the École des Beaux-Arts in Paris. They are screwing around in a studio, having fun being somewhat *outré*, in the grand tradition of French artists. The scene is an homage to a famous Rembrandt painting, *The Anatomy Lesson of Dr. Nicolaes Tulp* (1632). Rembrandt's subject—students crowding around a corpse being sliced open for their edification—was a popular one; many painters took it on before and after he did.

Doctors and artists share a focus on human anatomy; medical and art schools use skeletons to instruct. (Nice pom-pom on this one!) The corpses and skeletons came from sketchy sources with no regard for the consent of the "donors"—condemned criminals, hospitals for the poor, graveyards—and were almost always male. In all the many painted versions of the subject, there is nary a single woman, dead or alive.

Her presence here? She could be a friend or an artist herself, but most likely she was a model, who had just gotten dressed or was about to take off her clothes.

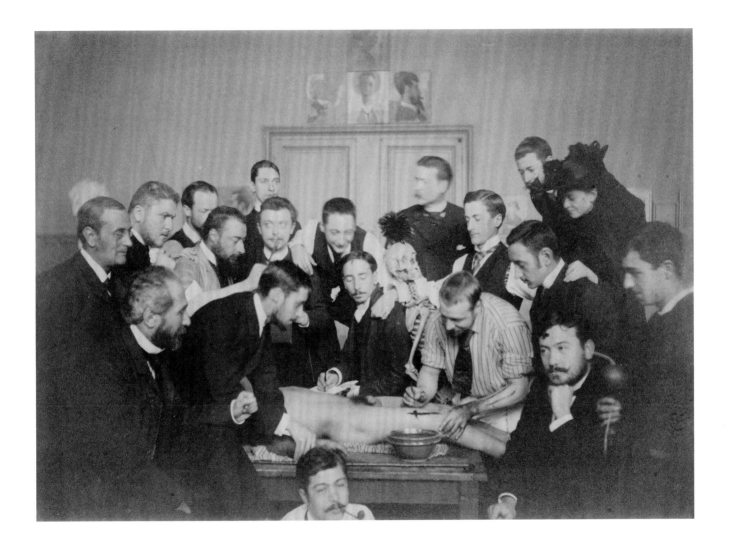

STELLA LEVY

Editorial Assistant
San Francisco, California, USA
1965

In the years since this moment was captured, it has accrued decades of associations and has become a bona fide iconic image, much reproduced and personally meaningful to many. This was San Francisco; this was the Beat movement at its holy place, the City Lights bookstore in North Beach, owned by the beloved poet Lawrence Ferlinghetti himself. There's Allen Ginsberg and Peter Orlovsky and, out of frame, even Bob Dylan. And yet despite the attention the photo has garnered, there has been scarce mention of the only woman pictured, nor was it considered in any way remarkable that she was only one.

Stella Levy was close friends with Allen Ginsberg and Peter Orlovsky at the time and it was Ginsberg who had recommended her to the bookstore manager for a job. Half a century later, Levy recalled the day thus: "The Poets' Pantheon is what the gathering in front of City Lights was called by the *Chronicle* newspaper, which published the photo by the gifted Larry Keenan. I was the first woman to work at City Lights, and then L.F. [Lawrence Ferlinghetti] hired me to be his first editorial assistant.

Lawrence pissed off a lot of the men by insisting that I stand with him in the photo. I don't know if any women poets were invited but none showed up. I was later able to get a job as the first woman hired at Moe's Bookstore in Berkeley and ditto at Bookstore Santa Cruz based on having worked at City Lights."[77]

"I am happy that other women followed me, most notably Nancy Peters. She and others convinced Ferlinghetti to make the bookstore a collective and today City Lights is still wonderful with women in charge of key positions. If you ever go there you will find the Poets Pantheon photo hanging high above a doorframe. Look up and I will wink at you." [78]

Stella has been a lifelong nonviolent social justice advocate who went on to an inspiring career as a labor lawyer and more recently founding an organization working to end the school-to-prison pipeline.

First row, L–R:
ROBERT LAVIGNE, SHIG MURAO, LEW WELCH, and PETER ORLOVSKY

Second row, L–R:
DAVID MELTZER, MICHAEL MCCLURE, ALLEN GINSBERG, DANIEL LANGTON, STEVE BORNSTEIN, GARY GOODROW (child in arms), RICHARD BRAUTIGAN (white hat), and LEYLAND MEYEZOVE (fur hat).

Third row, L–R:
STELLA LEVY, and LAWRENCE FERLINGHETTI

MARION CARPENTER

Photographer
Washington, D.C., USA
1947

In 1946 a Mr. Coffin, newspaper columnist, wrote about one of the very first American women White House press photographers, complaining that she "smiled and teased" to get her pictures. [79] When said photographer, Carpenter, saw the gentleman at lunch in the Senate dining room, she threw a bowl of bean soup at him to explain that she needed no feminine wiles to get her photos. Nobody caught the moment live, but she promptly posed in a reenactment shot—camera in one hand, soup plate in the other—which ran nationwide under the headline "Carpenter Nails Coffin." [80]

Carpenter was the first woman photographer to travel with a president (Truman), taking pictures daily. She is a little hard to see here, posing with the White House News Photographers Association, sitting on the lawn, left center, as Truman himself, an honorary member of the club, takes a picture. She later told friends that when an affair she was having with a married man was exposed, she was fired from her job at the White House.

She married a naval officer, left town with him, and ended up in the hospital from his abuse. She came back to D.C. to try to rebuild her career but ended up leaving town again, with a second husband, in another short marriage. She returned to her home in Saint Paul, Minnesota, where she worked as a nurse and took care of her son, her only child, and her mother. Years later, in 2002, she sadly died destitute and unknown, her body undiscovered for days. Recent efforts to honor her memory include an annual prize in her name given by the Saint Paul Camera Club.

CHRISTINE JORGENSEN

Entertainer and Trans Rights Advocate
New York, New York, USA
1953

She stands before the roiling sea of paparazzi, bestowing upon them her ruby lipstick and fabulous fur like a Hollywood starlet. But when Jorgensen arrived that day at New York's Idlewild Airport (now the John F. Kennedy International Airport), she was famous for one thing only: being the first American to publicly and successfully undergo gender confirmation surgery.

When she moved to Denmark three years earlier to seek the gender reassignment surgeries and hormone treatments as yet unavailable in the United States, she was a complete unknown from the Bronx in New York. Jorgensen did not crave the spotlight, but when her story got out before her return home, she had little choice: she made huge headlines around the world—stealing public attention from the polio vaccine, the Rosenberg trial, and the war in Korea—and she remains one of the best-known transgender people in history. She chose her name in honor of Christian Hamburger, the doctor who helped her become the woman she knew she always was.

In a letter to her parents when she told them her news, she wrote, "I've never been such a real person as I am today."[81]

Many expected her to perform, to entertain the masses that were loving the stream of photos of her doing even the most mundane things. Jorgensen did eventually craft a nightclub act in which she made up for her lack of musical abilities with charisma and charm. Her act was a hit—but at the same time, she was subject to daily hostility. The networks banned her from broadcast appearances, she was denied a marriage license, and she was the butt of endless cruel jokes.

In the 1960s, Jorgensen set off on a lecture tour around the country to talk to students about her life, generously sharing her story and answering a multitude of questions. Her goal for the tour was to break down the hatred and confusion around transness and provide a better world for future generations of trans people.

DIANA SPENCER

Teaching Assistant
London, England, UK
1980

Female royals have often been Only Women—in their public appearances they frequently entered all-male situations, from reviewing the troops to receiving foreign ministers to visiting coal mines and AIDS wards. A queen, a princess, or an empress in that sense does a very special "woman's job" that grants her an exceptional pass; her public function supersedes her gender in a way, granting a ceremonious superpower of entering male spaces that would otherwise be closed to women.

Diana came to embody another conception of an Only Woman: a lonely, abandoned woman, left unprotected, only one against many tormentors. She was beloved for how she allowed her personal vulnerability and fragility to contradict the power of her royalty and charisma. This image seems to conjure both her fragility and power.

On the one hand, she is facing the paparazzi alone, eye to eye with the photographer behind the lens, looking hunted and corralled on the street; on the other, she is on the verge of announcing the engagement that will define her life and make her a princess. Going royal, with all the powers that entails.

The image of being hounded by the paparazzi conjures other pictures and memories of a woman alone on the street surrounded by men: it is on a spectrum all the way from wolf whistles to sexual assault. The press presses in, with its phalanx of cameras.

Stretching down the sidewalk beyond her, we can make out a narrow path of escape, an untaken last exit, perhaps to a different future.

CHRISTINE LAGARDE

International Banker
Fukuoka, Japan
2019

Lagarde is here the only woman in an underrepresented role: the Boss. As president of the European Central Bank, a position she took up on November 1, 2019, she is addressed, at least in diplomatic circles, as Her Excellency. But this photograph commemorates an earlier occasion, in the spring of that year, when she appeared at the G20 Finance Ministers and Central Bank Governors Meeting, when she was still the managing director of the International Monetary Fund. Clearly, every man at this meeting knows exactly who she is, and she knows they know. She is French, chic, poised, confident, and direct, even from behind.

When Meryl Streep played the role of fashion-magazine editor Miranda Priestly in the film *The Devil Wears Prada*, she told *Variety* that she channeled "the unassailable elegance and authority of Christine Lagarde." [82]

As one of very few women at the top of her field of monetary policy and international finance and management, Lagarde has frequently been not only the Only Woman but also the First Woman in many of her jobs. She was the first and only woman to run the European Central Bank, the first and only woman to run the International Monetary Fund, the first French Minister of Finance, and the first female chair of a major international law firm. *Forbes* magazine has listed her among the ten most powerful women in the world every year since 2011, coming in at number two, behind only Angela Merkel, in 2019, and 2020.

BESSIE SMITH

Jazz Musician
Philadelphia, Pennsylvania, USA
c. 1920

I got the world in a jug, the stopper's in my hand. [83]
—"Down Hearted Blues," Bessie Smith's first hit

Smith turns the figure of the Only Woman upside down: she is the only woman because the stage is all hers! She was a revolutionary superstar; her backup dancers in dark matching suits are only there to underline her fabulous power.

In 1920 American music went crazy. A song by another blues singer, Mamie Smith's "Crazy Blues," begins as a broken-hearted lament but ends with the line "I'm going to get myself a gun and shoot myself a cop." [84] The first-ever recording by a Black woman, it sold astronomical numbers of copies and broke the culture wide open. Mamie Smith, the Queen of the Blues, was quickly joined by Ma Rainey, the Mother of the Blues; Bessie Smith, the Empress of the Blues; and a growing royal family of other funny, glamorous, and musically brilliant Black women singers. They had been working for years in Black entertainment before the recording industry started promoting them to Black and white audiences, who couldn't get enough.

Bessie Smith's first record sold three-quarters of a million copies and soon made her the highest-paid of all this sensational family. Dressing in pearls, diamonds, velvet, and silk, she dominated the stage and the scene. Openly bisexual, she merged masculine and feminine style, singing songs that layered tragedy, comedy, raunch, and irony. The music by women superstars in this era came to be known as classic blues. The scholar Daphne Duval Harrison has cataloged the radical and woman-centric subjects of their songs: "advice to other women; alcohol; betrayal or abandonment; broken or failed love affairs; death: departure; dilemma of staying with man or returning to family; disease and afflictions; erotica; hell; homosexuality; infidelity; injustice; jail and serving time; loss of lover; love; men; mistreatment: murder; other woman; poverty; promiscuity; sadness; sex; suicide; supernatural; trains; traveling: unfaithfulness; vengeance; weariness, depression and disillusionment; weight loss." [85]

Angela Davis sees Smith and her contemporaries as feminist revolutionaries who understood that the personal—the sexual—is political. Faced with "the vast disappointment that followed emancipation—when economic and political liberation must have seemed more unattainable than ever," Davis writes, these women "preached about sexual love, and . . . a collective experience of freedom, giving voice to the most powerful evidence there was for many black people that slavery no longer existed." [86]

By the end of the 1920s, the classic blues was dethroned by the country blues, embodied by the lone impoverished bluesman, the antithesis of showbiz and female glamour. And yet, many now trace the subsequent century of popular music—including Frank Sinatra, Elvis, Janis Joplin, and Beyoncé—directly back to the royal blueswomen who briefly flipped gender power relations upside down. [87]

CIXI

Empress
Bejing, China
1903

The only woman pictured here was born into an aristocratic family and began her political career at sixteen when she was brought to the Forbidden City, and selected by the Emperor as a third-grade concubine. Almost fifty years later, she poses in the splendid trappings of power, dripping with pearls from her headdress to her six-inch (fifteen-centimeter) platform horse-hoof shoes, in the Summer Palace in front of the Hall of Benevolence and Longevity, in one of her first-ever photographs, which she had taken as part of a canny public relations initiative.

Cixi was promoted to consort when she gave birth to the emperor's only son and heir in 1856, and, upon the emperor's death in 1861, she became empress dowager, along with his principal wife. The male figures carrying and surrounding her sedan chair are eunuchs, who served as servants, protectors, and counselors to power, and were not considered "real men." Old gossip painted her as wily in her pursuit of power from early on, bribing the eunuchs to get preferred access to the emperor's bed.

Cixi is an honorific that means "benevolent and auspicious," yet in popular memory and history, she has usually been called illiterate, corrupt, cruel, homicidal, and incompetent. Recent scholarship has, however, been uncovering new sources and stripping away encrusted layers of mythology and misogyny to enable fresh understanding of the woman who, through a series of coups, deaths, and mischief, ended up ruling China for forty-three years. In addition to having conflicting interpretations, her story holds intrinsic complexities and contradictions: she was perhaps *the* most powerful woman in the world, yet she was obliged to govern from behind an actual screen, and her own given name is lost to history, because a girl's name was not considered important enough to record.

Art historian Yuhang Li explains that Cixi was only able to rule in a deeply patriarchal society because of her prodigious ability to create an identity that, while very much female and her own, adapted traditional male aspects of power. According to Li, Cixi's agency is revealed through her greatest preoccupations, her artistic and religious practices: she "staged her sovereignty of female rulership" through her masterful understanding of different mediums, including not only photography, but also painting, Chinese opera, architecture, gardens, and even clothing, which were all intertwined with her lifelong worship of the goddess of mercy, Guanyin, who, in the Buddhist pantheon, had morphed from male to female. [88]

ETHEL BENJAMIN

Lawyer
Dunedin, New Zealand
1902

Deference and resentment can be so intimately inter-twined. The only woman here occupies the position of honor, centered among the gentlemen of the law in their robes and all their signifying accessories: top hats, wigs, starched collars, gloves, and watch chains. Almost to a man, these distinguished officers of the court are pulling long faces under their carefully groomed facial hair, while around her lips plays a little smile. That body language may only signify stereotypical gender presentation, but who's to say that her pleasure and their stony looks do not express the real story: her triumph and how they fought it all the way, for years, losing almost every battle.

Benjamin was an orthodox Jew, with an encouraging father, who finished secondary school with highest honors. In 1893 she became the first woman to enter law school in New Zealand; her colleagues, pictured here, wanted to deny her admission. They failed but probably took comfort in the fact that it was illegal for a woman to practice law. "Haha", she said with adroit Edwardian snark: "When I heard that being a woman I could not be admitted to the practise of the law, I was very indignant, and I suppose, being a true daughter of Eve, the fruit, because forbidden, became all the more attractive and desirable, and I grew all the more determined to follow the legal profession." [89]

While Benjamin was in school, Parliament fought over legalizing female practice, which some said would,

catastrophically, "desex" a woman. But the new law passed, in part due to her own growing and glowing reputation, just in time for graduation.

As Benjamin was first in her class, she was asked to speak—but only at the last minute. "I was somewhat diffident about taking so much upon myself at so short a notice. But I knew that little would be expected of me and even if I succeeded in talking nonsense, the charitable verdict would be, 'Oh well, it is all that can be expected of a woman.'" [90] When she set up her practice, her colleagues in town denied her entrance to the professional association, left her and only her out of their annual dinner, refused her any referral, tried to block her advertising, and sought to deny her the right to wear a wig. They wanted to invent a new costume, to handle this newfangled thing of a lady lawyer.

And so the little smile. She created an important practice in the face of that continuing harassment: she cofounded the local branch of the Society for the Protection of Women and Children and got deeply involved in cases of abuse, divorce, and adoption. Benjamin also represented rich women in their business deals, and she eventually became more of a businessperson herself. She married and moved to London, where by law she was once again barred from practicing.

MABEL GRIFFITH

Police Officer
Anaheim, California, USA
1927

This portrait of the police department in Anaheim depicts ten uniformed officers in the back row looking very much like troopers, and four people seated in the front looking like they're waiting for a bus. The woman in the pale print suit and the stylish bucket cloche is the town's first female police sergeant. Not that she would be in uniform, walking a beat. She was hired as a desk sergeant, and the *Santa Ana Register* wrote up her arrival: "Being arrested in Anaheim will now have its attractive points, because the first person to greet the new guests will be a charming, blonde-haired young woman." [91]

The chief, seated at the far right, explained that the department "should have a woman who would be able to handle the many affairs in which women are primarily interested, and furthermore," he said, "the department needed a complete bookkeeping and filing system which it has never had." Griffith, who was married to the town's personnel director, already had experience working in law offices.

Anaheim, which is world famous as the home of The Happiest Place on Earth, otherwise known as Disneyland, was then part of Los Angeles county and famous for its oranges.

VERA MENCHIK

Chess Champion
Karlovy Vary, Czechoslovakia
1929

The world's first women chess champion did not have an easy time of it. Seated here at a telling little remove from the rest, she is a newcomer, the only woman invited to play in the star-studded Carlsbad (as Karlovy Vary was then better known) tournament, considered to be among the strongest tournaments in the history of chess. Serious chess players of her era (coincidentally, men) tended toward the belief that constitutionally speaking, women couldn't be really good at chess and that they certainly had no business playing matches against the masters.

Before the matches, Austrian chess champion Johann Kmoch, for instance, declared he would go on stage as a ballerina if Menchik scored more than three points. (She scored three points.) Albert Becker, another swell playing in the contest, snarkily remarked that any player who lost to her would become a member of the Vera Menchik Club. Becker was the first to join said club, to be followed over time by eighteen other male chess masters. Alexander Alekhine, one of the greatest chess players of all time, covered the tournament for the *New York Times*. Of Menchik, he wrote: "After 15 rounds it is certain that she is an absolute exception in her sex. She is so highly talented for chess that with further work and experience at tournaments she will surely succeed in developing from her present stage of an average player into a high classed international champion. . . . It is the chess world's duty to grant her every possibility for development." [92]

Menchik was by all accounts a rather shy, calm, and awkward person. She was born in Moscow to a British mother and Bohemian father, both of whom worked for the nobility. Her father gave her a chess set when she was nine. The Russian Revolution had a damaging impact on her parents' employment, property, and marriage, and in 1921 her mother took Vera and her sister to England to live with their grandmother. Teenaged Vera, who spoke only Russian when she arrived, eventually made her way to the local chess club. She later described the game as "the best hobby for a person who cannot speak the language properly." [93] By 1925 she was the top female player in Britain. In 1927 she won the Women's World Championship, and she held the title of champion for seventeen years.

After Carlsbad, she played a tournament in Barcelona, later that year, where she was the first woman to win a prize in a master-level tournament. She continued to be invited to compete against men, but although she won games against masters and a couple of grandmasters, she never became a grandmaster herself. Tragically, when she was only thirty-eight, Vera, her sister, and her mother were all killed when their house in South London was bombed during World War II.

Activist and Educator
Washington, D.C., USA
1937

The only woman at the fifteenth annual Conference of Presidents of Negro Land Grant Colleges was neither a college president nor otherwise affiliated with the organization. The conference minutes describe her as a distinguished visiting speaker, whose address to the group took place just before this photo was taken at Howard University in Washington, D.C. Edwards' lecture was about African American students' study abroad: a why, what, and how on a subject about which she was deeply informed and personally passionate. She herself had just returned from Spain, where she was working to support the loyalists in the Civil War.

The granddaughter of an enslaved couple who ran away to Texas, Edwards was born there and lived in a number of places, from Chicago to Rome. She was an extraordinary figure who has not yet received the recognition she deserves. She is difficult to categorize, because she worked in so many different ways to help humanity: she was a teacher, social worker, journalist, feminist, labor activist, and protégé of the towering leader of the labor and civil rights movements, A. Philip Randolph. He helped her get a scholarship to study in Denmark.

Edwards traveled to the Soviet Union and Mexico, and extensively in Europe, developing her ideas and convictions about Pan-Africanism, socialism, and communism. She focused especially on the needs of children, women, and Black people, and worked to help resettle Jewish refugee children in Italy after World War II.

Conference of Presidents of Negro Land-Grant Colleges
15th Annual Convention, Nov 15-17 '37, Howard University
Washington, D.C. Scurlock, Photo.

GERTRUDE TREVELYAN

Writer
Oxford, England, UK
1933

Right in the center (like many of the women pictured in this book) is a young writer just on the heels of her successful, innovative first novel. She is gathered here with future members of Parliament and writers, fellow contributors to an anticommunist collection of essays titled *Red Rags: Essays of Hate from Oxford*.

G. E. Trevelyan, as she usually called herself on her books, had graduated from Oxford University in 1927 and was devoting herself to being a writer. She had exactly what Virginia Woolf said a woman writer needed: a room of her own (rented, in London) and £500 a year, enough to live on, nothing lavish. [94]

She spent the 1930s writing eight novels, each one quite different than the last. The first, *Appius and Virginia*, is the story of a woman who adopts an orangutan and raises him as a child, trying to create a human. Other books deal with young women at Oxford, a husband's psychological mistreatment of a wife, the desperation of unemployment, and formal experiments.

In October 1940, Trevelyan was injured when her flat in Notting Hill in London was hit in The Blitz. She died of her injuries soon after. Her death certificate bears the words "Spinster - Authoress." From there she disappeared from public view; her books fell out of print for almost eighty years. Thanks mostly to the creator of the website Neglected Books, a new edition of *Appius and Virginia* was released in 2020 to fresh interest and appreciation.

MIA WESTERLUND ROOSEN

Sculptor
New York, New York, USA
1982

I think of my pieces as bodies. [95]

—Mia Westerlund Roosen

In a gathering of radicals that went on to become canonical, are some of the artists represented by the legendary art dealer Leo Castelli, who is seated seemingly in the air right in the middle. They're celebrating the twenty-fifth anniversary of his fantastically successful gallery, at lunch at the Odeon Restaurant, smushed into the space in the basement outside the bathrooms where patrons self-served tons of cocaine (it was the 1980s). They're all fairly touchy-feely and cozy, with Robert Rauschenberg holding Andy Warhol's injured wrist, but Westerlund Roosen is naturally the only one being embraced, we hope happily.

A sculptor who began working with naturalistic forms in the 1960s when Minimalism was all the rage, Westerlund Roosen was one of only a handful of women who Castelli represented. Throughout her long career, she has been making beguiling works in a great number of materials and phases, which often refer to the body and other organic shapes. From stupendously big to small, her sculptures tend to "show the hand of their maker" and have a strong sensuous appeal.

She says that she certainly wants her work to be seen as feminist, "but the only way I feel that can be relayed to a viewer is to make the work intensely female. Who knows if that's achievable." [96]

Represented since 2006 by the Betty Cuningham Gallery, she cites another unifying aspect of her somehow subversive art: "I think all of my work is a bit Dadaist, a little humorous." [97] Droopy, perky, thrusting, bouncy, disarming, the works are indeed sometimes laugh out loud funny—in addition to their other qualities of sensuality, beauty, and curiosity.

Standing, L-R:
ELLSWORTH KELLY, DAN FLAVIN, JOSEPH KOSUTH, RICHARD SERRA, LAWRENCE WEINER, NASSOS DAPHNIS, JASPER JOHNS, CLAES OLDENBURG, SALVATORE SCARPITTA, RICHARD ARTSCHWAGER, CLETUS JOHNSON, <u>MIA WESTERLUND ROOSEN</u>, and KEITH SONNIER.

Seated, L-R:
ANDY WARHOL, ROBERT RAUSCHENBERG, LEO CASTELLI, EDWARD RUSCHA, JAMES ROSENQUIST, and ROBERT BARRY.

JESSIE BOYD SCRIVER

Medical Student
Montreal, Canada
1920

She's right in the front and center, but unlike almost all the men—and the boy—she is looking down. She doesn't appear to share the mood of her medical school classmates.

In 1918, two years before this photo was taken, Scriver was accepted into McGill University Medical School as part of a special initiative in response to wartime conditions. So many doctors, and so many young men, had left home for Europe to serve in World War I, that the city of Montreal was short on both doctors and medical students. McGill decided as a one-time measure to admit four women as "partial students," a hitherto unknown status.

She wasn't warmly welcomed: some of her classmates even picketed her family home, and, in an anatomy class, they threw bloody organs at her. Nevertheless, after a year she won full-time regular status, and went on to graduate second in her class. She became Montreal's exceedingly accomplished first woman pediatrician. An expert in sickle cell anemia and premature infants, she served as head of the Canadian Paediatric Society and retained a faculty post at McGill until she died in 2000 at the age of 105.

A shortage of men, due to war or other causes, is a well-established way that women have gained entrance to public life.

ELIZABETH BARTHOLET

Law Professor
Cambridge, Massachusetts, USA
1987

This photograph was taken in the same academic year that Michelle Obama (then Robinson) graduated from Harvard Law School; these were her professors. Not all of them made it to the faculty class photo that day, but the picture pretty much tells the story.

The faculty was all white men for over 150 years, and cracking that hold has been a long, bumpy, and continuing road. The first Black person to win tenure was Derrick Bell in 1971, followed over ten years later by two more Black men, including Charles Ogletree on the upper right. Bartholet was the first woman "to survive the tenure process," as she put it. [98] Then in 1990, Bell, in protest, refused to teach until the school finally appointed a Black woman. Two years later Harvard fired him! *Six years later*, the Law School finally recruited the first tenured Black woman, Lani Guinier. In 2021 the tenured faculty was 22 percent women.

But in this book, the number of greatest interest is the number one, and the commitment of Harvard Law School to the phenomenon of Onliness was deep, as can be seen in the annual faculty photos, which have a persistent pattern of one woman at a time.

Five different women each appear alone for one, two, or three years, over a forty-year period. Each Only Woman's presence was punctuated by years of all maleness, a kind of reset.

The first woman ever pictured in the group was a visiting professor in 1947 and 1948. Then back to all men. A second Only Woman in 1951 and 1953. Eleven years of all men again, then a third appears for a record three years in a row. She is replaced by a fourth for a year, and then in 1971 appears a fifth Only Woman. Admittedly, not every faculty member showed up for the annual pictures, but still, the first sighting of *two* women is in 1979, thirty-two long years after the First. Bartholet in 1988 is the last sighting of an Only in the annual Harvard Law Faculty photos; the next year staff members were invited in, and thus—in the category of "woman," at least—the "none or the only one" became history.

ELLEN SWALLOW RICHARDS

Environmental Chemist
Cambridge, Massachusetts, USA
1900

The only woman here, among chemistry staff at the Massachusetts Institute of Technology (MIT), was a First and a visionary. She devoted herself not only to science but also to connecting ordinary women and science. She brought to the United States the idea of ecology, which she planted firmly in domestic life. She was a pioneer in public health and consumer safety, exposing and campaigning against pollutants and dangers in food, air, water, and public school buildings. At various times she used the terms *euthenics*, *human ecology*, *home economics*, and *science of right living* to try to describe her vision of a living system, with the home in close relation to science, nature, and society—as well as the political potential of a woman's movement to effect change in those realms. She saw her work as a way to liberate and empower women who were often caged in the domestic sphere. [99]

She began her studies at Vassar College, then a new all-women school, where she was a voracious student of the astronomer Maria Mitchell. She subsequently became MIT's first woman student, graduating in the class of 1873. A biographer discovered that MIT in fact let her in as "an experiment" that was explicitly set up to fail. [100]

The administrators wanted her to be the exception that proved the rule—the rule being that women were incapable of higher education. An observer of a faculty meeting said "she was put on trial for all women." She was kept in an isolated lab, like a "dangerous animal." [101]

In diaries and letters Richards explained that in response to this treatment, she made a deliberate effort to make herself helpful in distinctly feminine ways to the all-male faculty, sewing buttons and sweeping up for them in an ingratiation campaign. She also served as lab assistant, and between her two types of services, she held her footing. When her advancement was blocked, she pivoted, raised money, and convinced the institute to let her establish a chemistry laboratory—for women students only.

CLARISSA WIMBUSH

Dentist
Alexandria, Virginia, USA
1961

Dr. Clarissa Wimbush was the only woman member, as well as president for a term, of the Old Dominion Dental Society (ODDS), an organization of Black dentists in Virginia that was founded in 1913. She was the first Black woman dentist in the state; the first in the United States was Ida Gray, who began her practice in 1890. However, the first First must usually be followed by many more Firsts until they are no longer worth noting: that is, the first in the country in 1890, the first in Virginia almost fifty years later, and so on and on.

Dr. Clarissa, as she was called, was short in stature, often standing on a box to treat patients, and was a dynamo who had a thriving practice taking care of Black and white people for fifty years, in spite of obstacles, such as being refused a bank loan to set it up. She was greatly concerned about issues of access and making sure that her patients would be well taken care of after she retired.

In 2021 ODDS still exists, and the second woman president is Dr. Lori Wilson, the exuberant author of a book about the history of Black women dentists. Dr. Wilson has said that she finds this photo deeply inspirational and moving, pointing out that white hotels in Virginia at that time refused Black guests, so when ODDS members came together in their annual conference, they often stayed with local African American families who opened up their homes. They were likewise barred from the national association of dentists, which remained officially all white until 1965. [102] Meanwhile, she explained, Black folks really needed their own dentists, since that was the only way most were going to be able to access care. Every member of the society likely showed up for annual meetings: "it was one hundred percent participation," and they were important community events, with parades and hired entertainers, such as Cab Calloway and Count Basie. [103]

Dr. Wilson imagines it must have been tough for Dr. Wimbush; she says that the profession is "still male dominated, and some of the things that women in the profession have to deal with are just not visible to the men." Even being addressed as "doctor," for example, is still something women need to insist upon, a problem that male colleagues don't have. [104]

FLORENCE NORTH

Boxing Promoter
New York, New York, USA
1922

The newspaper caption that originally ran with this photo highlights the shock of a woman being a boxing promoter, while offering a solution to the mystery of how it works: the fighters "do their darndest in every bout, for a woman's tongue is a thing of fury." [105] North got a lot of attention for her move into boxing, but she didn't stay in the business long—it seems she had bigger fish to fry.

Zelda Fitzgerald, wife of novelist F. Scott Fitzgerald and the glamorous embodiment of the 1920s liberated woman, described the figure thus: "The Flapper awoke from her lethargy of sub-deb-ism, bobbed her hair, put on her choicest pair of earrings and a great deal of audacity and rouge and went into the battle . . . she refused to be bored chiefly because she wasn't boring. . . . She had mostly masculine friends, but youth does not need friends—it needs only crowds." [106]

North was a flapper with a gift for publicity and a nose for action. She was twenty-five, a recent law school grad, and within months she reappeared all over the papers, across the country, in a brand new identity as the "Girl Sleuth" promising to solve a notorious double murder in New Jersey. The victims were a married church choir member and her equally married minister, who'd been carrying on so obviously that they got carried away—by someone with a knife *and* a gun.

North jumped in as a volunteer to represent the choir singer's sixteen-year-old daughter, who "needed a woman's counsel, a lawyer's skill and a detective's brain. I have tried to give her all of these. I am first a woman, with a tender sympathy for her." [107]

The minister's wife—an heiress—was the obvious suspect, but as North boldly proclaimed, the police bungled the case so badly it could never be officially solved. North may have sold the juicy love letters of the victims to the press for $500. In any case, she was quoted daily in newspapers around the country for months and months, before disappearing from the scene, leaving the rest of her life story another unsolved mystery. The word "moxie" hadn't come into use yet, but it springs to mind for North.

JANET GUTHRIE

Race Car Driver
Trenton, New Jersey, USA
1976

Ace auto racer Guthrie is shown here surrounded by her fellow racers, who are looking congenial and sharing a magazine. But appearances can be less complicated than the truth.

Guthrie started flying planes at thirteen and made her first parachute jump at sixteen. After a college love affair with physics, she started out as an engineer in aviation, buying herself a nice little car to drive to work. She ended up getting deeply involved with that stunning 1953 Jaguar XK120 M coupe, learning its mechanics inside out and even sleeping in it. Before long she was racing, first in a Jaguar XK140. Eventually, she started racing full-time, track after track for race after race. She was the first woman to qualify for and compete in the top two US races, the Indianapolis 500 and the Daytona 500, and made history again and again. The tyranny of sponsorship and money—and equipment—was her biggest obstacle, one that, as she pointed out from retirement in 2020, still blocks women from competing. [108]

When she started, she was entering a *real* good ol' boys' club. While pioneering the sport for women with bravery and skill, she was constantly subjected to nasty, persistent sexism from the drivers, fans, and press. But over time, she noticed a shift. In 2010 she observed that "there has been a big change in reaction to me. The hostility has cooled down quite a bit. I think the worst is over. The initial reaction to me was one of a lack of respect. . . . What I'm trying to emphasize is that a driver is primarily a person, not a man or a woman." [109]

ANDREA MOTLEY CRABTREE

US Army Deep Sea Diver
Panama City, Florida, USA
1982

"I love that photo," said retired Master Sergeant Andrea Motley Crabtree with a laugh, thirty-nine years after it was taken. "For me, it captures everything. Most of the men hated me being there. The way he's looking at me with such disgust! He didn't make it. He was claustrophobic. He couldn't understand how I was better than him."

After five years in the US Army Motley entered the military diving school which is run by the Navy. Of some thirty students who entered in 1982, only eleven made it through, including Motley. She became the first woman deep sea diver for the army, and the first Black woman in US military diving, capable of welding underwater and using heavy equipment in underwater construction and salvage operations.

Motley, whose suit in the photo weighed two hundred pounds (91 kilograms), was a natural. "I'm a Pisces. I didn't have any fear. I'm not trying to brag, but I was a good diver." She felt at home underwater, where a mysterious pull on her fin might turn out to be a playful otter, or an enormous merchant marine ship loomed over her head, emitting a whole-body vibrating hum.

The grueling training and the actual work were the easy parts. Trouble started at graduation when a local reporter misquoted her as saying she had to overcome three strikes: being a woman, Black, and Army in a Navy facility. What she had actually said was was that she *feared* those strikes being counted against her, but had in fact been fairly treated. Nevertheless her command called her ungrateful, a publicity hound making false accusations of prejudice and mistreatment.

She was soon sent to South Korea, where although the Master Diver in charge taught her volumes and remains a good friend decades later, "most of these guys—they felt that if a woman could do what they were doing, then they weren't as badass as they thought they were." She recalled that "Nobody ever came up to me and said point blank, 'We don't like Black people.' But men were telling me all the time that they didn't think women should be divers." Hazing and intimidation included constant sexist comments, gags like snakes in the freezer, and uglier stuff, such as playing with her air when she was two hundred feet (61 meters) underwater.

But all that was water off the proverbial duck. Things really went wrong with a new supervising Master Diver, and when the job of diver was reclassified and closed to women. Instead of sending her to a coveted training slot at the next level, the Army sent a man with lower rank and less experience. The sexism eventually drove her away and still stings: "I was a good diver. Why wasn't that enough?" [110]

ANNA FRANSEN LA MONTAGNE

Goldminer
Fairbanks, Alaska, USA
c. 1900

Sometimes we can know all the facts of a life and still know very little. Fransen was born to Danish immigrant parents in Washington State. For unknown reasons, she ended up in Fairbanks, Alaska, where, at the age of twenty-one in 1909, she married a handsome Quebecois gold miner named George La Montagne.

Her husband had been drawn west ten years before by the gold rush, working in the Klondike and Nome before settling in Fairbanks and working for famed gold miner Felix Pedro, whose find in 1902 started the stampede. Pedro died in 1910, possibly poisoned by his wife, and George staked his own claim, on what was called Goldstream No. 17.

He is seen here on his wife's left, arms crossed, in front of the shed-like structure attached to the building that seals in warmth, known as an "arctic entry". At that time, women could not yet vote, nor were they legally able to stake a claim.

Photographs of the young couple show them with their dog sled, and in one captioned "Clean Up," Anna is all dressed up with four other ladies and all the men in suits at the camp. So there were other fancy ladies, but they didn't regularly hang out at the camp. Perhaps Anna was working there, helping to feed the men, or visiting for photo ops.

Luck soon began to turn on Fairbanks, with a sharp decline in gold: 1911 yielded half the amount of 1909, and the young family sold out and moved to Seattle, where the 1930 census describes Anna as a housewife and George the gold miner as a "poultry man." [111]

UNION MINING CO No 17 GOLD STREAM

Huey Photo

KATHARINE GRAHAM

Publisher
New York, New York, USA
1975

Graham was a First as well as an Only. In the instance of this photograph, she was the first woman elected to the Associated Press's board of directors. She sits here as the sole spot of color in light blue with the other directors, all visibly pale and male.

Three years earlier, she had already become the first female CEO of a Fortune 500 company, the *Washington Post,* which her father, Eugene Meyer, had bought in 1933. When he quit the job of publisher in 1946 to become president of the World Bank, Meyer gave it to his son-in-law, Phil, a lawyer. Graham, who had worked for a paper in San Francisco as well as for the *Post,* did not mind—in fact, as she later wrote in her autobiography, "It never crossed my mind that he might have viewed me as someone to take on an important job at the paper." [112] And so it was that when he gave the couple ownership of the company's shares, he gave Phil 70 percent and Katharine 30.

But then Phil died in 1963, and so she became the boss. Not that she was brimming with confidence and champing at the bit. Indeed, in 1969 she said, "I think a man would be better in the job I'm in than a woman." [113]

Nevertheless, she took the company public, kept it profitable, and made journalistic history in the fight against government secrecy. In 1971 she gave her paper the go-ahead to publish the Pentagon Papers, which brought to light the scope of US failed policy and involvement in the Vietnam War, and then to investigate the Nixon administration's illegal efforts to reelect the president, which ultimately brought about Nixon's forced resignation and numerous government reforms.

MARGARET THATCHER

Politician
London, England, UK
1979

Thatcher, who had just become the first woman prime minister of the United Kingdom, poses with her new cabinet in the Pillared Room at Number 10 Downing Street, a replica of a sixteenth-century Persian rug under her feet and a ghostly Joshua Reynolds painting of a real English lady above her head. She herself was to become, for better or for worse, a kind of embodiment of Britishness, a female figure almost as potent as the queen herself. She was also a classic type of Only Woman.

She adored her father, who was a grocer; in her eight-hundred-page autobiography she never mentioned her mother even once. She married up and went further up than even she could have imagined. "I don't think there will be a woman prime minister in my lifetime," she said when she was education secretary, a mere six years before this photo was taken. [114]

Thatcher, like Indira Gandhi and Golda Meir—the two most powerful female prime ministers on this planet who took office before she did—was dubbed the "Iron Lady." All three received the same compliment from a different male wag in each country, who remarked that she was the "only man" in her all-male cabinet (i.e., she was more decisive, effective, brave, and so on, than her colleagues, a true man among their womanishness).

She seemed to prefer being the only woman among men and was often called a "Queen Bee," using the metaphor of a single powerful woman who keeps other females down (albeit an inaccurate version of bee society). In her eleven years as prime minister, she only appointed one woman to her cabinet, never promoted any Tory women members of Parliament, and never championed any so-called women's issues.

One of her aides expressed her attitude with concision: while "she rather liked men (preferring our company, perhaps, to that of women), she thought us the weaker sex." She often boasted of the superiority of women, uttering Thatcherisms like "In politics, if you want anything said ask a man, if you want anything done ask a woman." [115] But she may well have been referring only to herself.

ABIGAIL HOFFMAN

Hockey Player
Toronto, Canada
1956

The player in the front row, second from the left, was pretty good, especially on defense. The coach thought Ab Hoffman was sometimes a little rough with opponents but skilled enough to make the league all-star team after months slicing up the ice with the TeePees. Under the all-star team rules, all ages had to be double-checked against birth certificates, and that's when the cat leapt out of the bag. A huge headline in the *Toronto Daily Star* in March 1956 blared, "Girl, 9, Hockey League Star Never Spotted Among 400 Boys." The head youth hockey official said of the discovery, "It completely knocked the wind right out of me." [116]

Hoffman appeared with her parents and teammates in newspapers, radio interviews, and a documentary film, explaining that she'd shown her birth certificate when she first signed up but nobody had noticed her gender. She had been skating since she was three and just wanted to play. There was no girls' team. But her parents saw no reason boys and girls couldn't play together, so they had kept mum. She was allowed to finish the season, but that was it. Girls' teams that existed before the war had died out by the 1950s, while organized hockey for boys had exploded in popularity. After the media frenzy about Hoffman, there was talk of starting a girls' league—ninety girls showed up to register—but the effort faded out.

Hoffman's fame only grew over her lifetime. At fourteen she won the national championship in the 880-yard race, and went on to run in four Olympics and win gold medals in the Pan American and Commonwealth Games. She became a sports administrator and lifelong advocate for amateur and women athletes. In the mid-1980s, there was another story very like her own, but this time the girl player sued, charging discrimination. Hoffman supported her and she won the case.

SARAH FULLER

Football Player
Nashville, Tennessee, USA
2020

In 2020 the football team at Vanderbilt University in Nashville, Tennessee, was in trouble: COVID-19 had knocked out so many players that the team was short. Although there is no place more off-limits to women than an American football field, the coach of the Commodores turned in desperation to Fuller, a star player on the women's soccer team, for help. When she stepped in to assist, she became the first woman to play at the top level of college football and the first to score. At the same time, she joined the many other women in history who entered previously all-male public spaces when calamity limited the number of available men.

Sporting a helmet that reads "Play Like a Girl," the six-feet-one-inch (nearly two-meter) –tall athlete became an instant star to a sports-hungry, pandemic-weary country.

Fuller's new teammates nicknamed her "Champ," and she was soon appearing on television. She was even picked to introduce the first-ever woman vice president, Kamala Harris, at the 2021 presidential inauguration ceremony.

Up until the end of middle school, Fuller was always the tallest kid—boy or girl—in her class, a vantage point that she relished. She began playing soccer at age five. Fuller says that while playing with the Commodores, she wasn't treated any differently than the men, and she felt confident that her remarkable kicking skills "brought value" to the team. But asked what she would tell younger women athletes, she said, "Women belong in the sports world and they have amazing strength. But be prepared and aware of the inequalities. It's not all rainbows and butterflies." [117]

MARGARET NAYLOR

Diver
Tobermory Bay, Scotland, UK
1924

The newspapers loved the only woman pictured here; they called her the "Girl in the Iron Pajamas" and couldn't get enough of her story. The daughter of a Scottish vicar, Naylor began diving during World War I when she went to work for the British Navy Department. According to a reporter for the *Hamilton Evening Journal*, "She did remarkable work on some of the sunken warships, and became recognized as the leading diver of Europe, male or female." [118]

Naylor ended up working for a Col. Kenneth Mackenzie Foss, who had long been obsessed with recovering a legendary sunken treasure off the coast of Scotland. A Spanish galleon limping home in 1588 after the humiliating defeat of the Spanish Armada spent over a month at anchor in Tobermory Bay before she exploded and sank. The cause of the explosion is as murky as the silt she slowly sank further into; it may have been the work of some Scots who didn't want to see her sail away—laden as she was thought to be with gold and even, in some tellings, a crown for the expected Spanish king of England.

Foss began his search efforts in 1909, putting together various companies and dives, retrieving just enough—a gold ring, candlesticks—to keep hope alive through interruptions of war and injury. By 1919 he'd recruited Naylor, who tried unsuccessfully to deploy a fire-hose-type contraption to help uncover the wreck. Here she is preparing to try again, to no avail.

The last trace of her diving career is found in 1926, when an American newspaper reports that Britain has gone to the birds: "Women, Women, Everywhere in British Trade: Feminine Invasion Complete." Warning that "British women have successfully invaded every masculine occupation but that of fatherhood," the article explains: "Many of them are pretty. . . . Some are married. Some are 'surplus women'—the men who might have been their husbands buried on European battlefields." They are suddenly appearing everywhere, as doctors, factory owners, explorers, pilots—even a deep sea diver, "angling off the coast . . . for treasure." [119]

ETHEL "SUNNY" LOWRY

Swimmer
Folkestone, England, UK
1960

When Lowry was a student at Manchester High School for Girls, the headmistress peered sternly at her from over half-moon glasses and said, "Lowry, what is your ambition?" to which she immediately replied, "To swim the channel." "Dismissed," her headmistress said, without another word. [120]

Lowry's father was a fish wholesaler who knew a thing or two about the life aquatic, so he encouraged her to train for her ambition to swim the English Channel. This she did, choosing as her trainer Jabez Wolffe, who put her on a high-protein diet (which included forty eggs a week) and an arduous training schedule of three or four hours a day.

Wolffe himself had tried and failed to swim the Channel twenty-two times and thwarted Gertrude Ederle's first attempt by pulling her from the water prematurely. So it was perhaps no surprise that Lowry's first attempt—from England to France, in August 1932—was foiled by strong east–west currents, while Wolffe and Captain Courtez of the support tug *Isobelle* spent forty-five minutes trying to find her before lightning flashes lit up her red swimming cap.

The following July, she made her second attempt, changing direction to allow the current to help her, but once again was unsuccessful. That August, however, in her third attempt, the twenty-two-year-old Lowry swam from Cap Gris-Nez in France to St. Margaret's Bay, Dover, in fifteen hours, forty-one minutes.

The deciding factor may very well have been the strong-willed Lowry's decision to cast off the traditional heavy wool one-piece swimsuit and wear instead a daring, lighter two-piece suit, for which she was labeled a "harlot" for baring her knees. [121]

Before she died at the age of ninety-seven, Lowry was inducted into the International Marathon Swimming Association's Hall of Fame, and at ninety-four she was awarded an MBE for services to swimming in England's North West region. The Dover Museum's *Swimming the Channel* exhibition features a rather bedraggled looking red woolen two-piece, perfect for a national heroine, and a harlot.

JOANN MORGAN

Space Engineer
Cape Canaveral, Florida, USA
1969

Morgan was twenty-eight years old and the only woman in the Kennedy Space Center's firing room among nearly five hundred men when Apollo 11 took off for its trip to the moon in 1969. Here you can just make her out in the third row, to the right center. Her inclusion in the room for liftoff was an issue. "I didn't know it at the time—I learned this later—but it was a big discussion that went all the way up to the Kennedy Space Center director." [122]

Morgan started young, with a father who gave her a chemistry set and didn't mind when she blew up the patio. She was a high achiever who found male mentors, encouraging bosses, and a supportive husband, who all helped her rip through career milestones. She also faced opposition, from outright efforts to exclude, to harassment that included persistent obscene phone calls from anonymous colleagues—which she never reported.

The precocious start, supportive family or mentors, and ongoing resistance and harassment are all hallmarks of the First experience. And Morgan is a classic First: first female engineer and first female executive at the Kennedy Space Center, and recipient of countless awards over her forty-five years at NASA. She appeared in so many photographs as the Only that she became used to it. In the late 1970s, she finally began to notice that she was no longer almost *always* the only woman in the room.

"My wish would be, all the photos in the future, there will always be women," she said. "Not just one woman—there will be women." [123]

BONNIE DUNBAR

Astronaut
Mir Space Station
1998

Dunbar, the seventh American woman in space, became one of the most experienced NASA astronauts, flying on five space shuttle missions between 1985 and 1998, including two dockings with the Mir Space Station. Here, on her fifth and final space flight, she poses with her American and Russian colleagues in their microgravity environment. As payload commander, Dunbar was in charge of twenty-three science and tech experiments.

She grew up on a cattle ranch in Washington state, where she was "on a horse before I could walk" and driving a tractor by age nine, she recalls in an interview in an oral history series, the Legacy Project. Dunbar first applied to work at NASA when she was eighteen. NASA told her to go to college, so in 1967 she became the first person in her family to do so, majoring in ceramic engineering. She later wrote her PhD thesis about physiology in space, and she became an educator after her retirement from NASA.

In the interview, she describes the moment when the engines cut upon entry into orbit: "Suddenly you drop from three times your body weight to zero. You're immediately in a weightless environment—freefalling around Earth. You're still strapped into your seat, but ... This checklist ... for example, starts floating up. It won't float away. It's tethered. But its pages are flapping about as if there was wind. So, you know you're in a different environment. Then you look out the window and you see a *really* different environment. The Earth is passing below you."

When interviewer Trova Heffernan asked Dunbar what issues she faced in the field as a woman, Dunbar simply said, "I never saw them." She added, "I know that sounds hard to believe, and they may have been out there.... Either I selectively decided not to hear, or I always looked at it as a challenge." [124]

CLARA A. PRATT

Botanist
Niagara Glen, Canada
1924

In August 1924 the annual meeting of the British Association for the Advancement of Science took place in Toronto. The group dubbed "Section K: Botany" seems to have been granted license to take off for a weekend to Niagara Glen, "where a canvas camp had been prepared for us by military authorities. Saturday was mainly devoted to a botanical ramble through the dense woods which line both sides of the gorge. The area is a government reserve, but Section K was permitted to botanize." [125]

The only woman here, who is so enjoying her barbecued mushrooms on a stick, was the author that year of the paper "The Staling of Fungal Cultures" and a lecturer at Imperial College, London. Pratt, a specialist in plant geography and economic botany, worked at the college for thirty-three years. According to a history of the college, she "conducted research around the world," and one hopes that it was often as much fun as she seems to be having here. [126]

ELAINE DE KOONING

Painter
Black Mountain, North Carolina, USA
1948

Officially, de Kooning was a "faculty wife" at Black Mountain College, tagging along with her painter husband, Willem, when he was brought in as a last-minute substitute teacher. The thirty-year-old de Kooning (née Fried) was already a serious artist, but she took advantage of the summer opportunity to be a student, taking classes from Merce Cunningham, R. Buckminster Fuller, and Josef Albers.

Black Mountain College, founded in 1933 in response to the Nazi shutdown of the Bauhaus in Germany, became a legendary place for artists over its twenty-four years of existence. Pictured here is Fuller (background, right)—dedicated to improving society through architecture and technology, like his Bauhaus predecessors—looking on as de Kooning and his other young students try to build his first large-scale geodesic dome. Unfortunately, since he could only afford half of the necessary materials, the dome failed—hence its name: Supine Dome.

As de Kooning's practice unfolded, she remained deeply committed to Abstract Expressionism but became best known for her portraiture, which combined abstraction and figuration in a deeply personal way. She was commissioned to paint John F. Kennedy's portrait, as her quick, action-oriented style suited the restless president.

She didn't see significant obstacles facing women artists—she got on with things, with her characteristic artistic and social energy. The sixteen-painting series she created at Black Mountain College was found rolled up in her studio upon her death in 1989.

FRIDA KAHLO

Artist
Mexico City, Mexico
1929

Twenty-two-year-old Kahlo appears here as a revolutionary comrade and the lover of Diego Rivera, as he leads the contingent of painters and sculptors among the arts workers on a May Day march. The pair married in August of that year, which made her instantly well known, as in "Diego and Frida," or as her mother saw them, elephant and dove. [127] Was she in his shadow, or—as Elaine de Kooning said of being married to her own more famous painter husband—was she in his light?

One reason for the enduring interest in Kahlo's presentation of self is the way she mixed aspects of masculine and feminine so unexpectedly and idiosyncratically. Her self-portraits usually show her decked out in her signature folkloric garb of *Mexicanidad*, in bright colors and flowers, under a fierce unibrow and mustache.

Here she is in more masculine garb, with a worker's cap in hand, dressed not as she painted herself, but in the severe uniform of the devoted militant she was all her life. She is ramrod straight, suffering the chronic pain from her terrible bus accident and its consequences. Her position as Rivera's partner, her revolutionary commitment, extraordinary courage, and refusal to bow to convention gave her entrée into male space over her short life. She was also seductive, carrying on with many male and female lovers, including Isamu Noguchi and Leon Trotsky.

She loved the camera, as the many photos of her attest. Her father was a photographer, and here she seems aware of the camera, which was held by her friend, the Italian leftist and feminist Tina Modotti. We are used to seeing her as the "only woman" in another sense, in her endlessly inventive self-portraits that picture her alone. In those portraits, she took herself seriously, enough to focus intensely on her own self and pain.

MARTHA GELLHORN

War Correspondent
Cassino, Italy
1944

I only loved the world of men—not the world of men-and-women. I only loved the men as they were themselves, not as they became in relation to women. Perhaps I am simply a born visitor—meant to go, as a stranger, into someone else's territory, having none of my own. [128]

—Martha Gellhorn, in a 1958 letter

On D-Day—the June 6, 1944, Allied invasion of Normandy —150,000 men and exactly one woman hit the beaches and tried to make it alive onto French soil. That woman was Gellhorn, an American journalist who was in England when her accreditation to travel with the troops was suddenly withdrawn. Determined to go, she slipped onto a hospital ship, claiming she was doing a story on the nurses. She locked herself in a bathroom and stowed away until she managed to disembark with the medics, carrying a stretcher under fire and finding her way inland with the soldiers who made it. [129]

Gellhorn covered every conflict in her lifetime, from the Spanish Civil War onward, including World War II and the liberation of the Dachau concentration camp, the Japanese invasion of China, the US war in Vietnam, and, in her eighties, the US invasion of Panama. An all-time-great war correspondent, she began by covering poverty during the Great Depression. She said that her approach to war was formed then: while her male colleagues rushed to the front, she made a point of lagging behind, writing about those left behind in the carnage.

Gellhorn lived in a man's world and had many relationships with celebrated and beguiling men, but always felt that she failed at love and sex. [130] Her first husband was

Bertrand de Jouvenel, who had previously had a long sexual relationship with his stepmother, Colette. Later she met Ernest Hemingway, who was soon off to Spain, as one of thousands of global volunteers joining the fight against Fascism. She went too—and eventually married him, leading to another kind of conflict, fully dramatized by Nicole Kidman in a cheesy movie.

The caption of this photo of her at work on the Italian front just months before D-Day, typed by US Army personnel, reads, "Mrs. Hemingway takes her first look at Cassino." Ernest cabled her, "Are you a war correspondent or a wife in my bed?" [131] It turned out that her press credentials were yanked right before D-Day because Ernest, by then her ex, convinced her magazine to send him instead of her, simply to spite her. She left him and deeply resented having her name tied to his ever after.

Gellhorn wrote nonfiction books and novels, and her letters have also been published. The writer Fintan O'Toole describes them as "precious traces of the turbulent, passionate, relentless, self-examined inner life of a woman of honor whose indomitable character is beautifully summed up by her mother . . . : 'She lacks everything that makes living easy, she possesses most things that make it worthwhile.'" [132]

UNKNOWN

Railroad Worker
Pennsylvania, USA
c. 1942–44

Piloting a motor car in a Pennsylvania Railroad yard was one of the "war jobs" that suddenly opened up when millions of American men were sent overseas between 1940 and 1945. Women, minorities, people with disabilities, and others who'd been excluded from the labor market poured into the jobs. "Rosie the Riveters" were often earning decent wages for the first time in their lives. As always, the experiences of workers differed widely by identity, but the female labor force grew by fifty percent; six hundred thousand "Black Rosies" entered defense industry jobs; and the number of women working as domestics declined sharply.

The woman here is unidentified, but others reminiscing in the 1990s about their Pennsylvania Railroad war jobs spoke mostly fondly about the experience. It was fun, challenging work and good money. Kay Dworchak, a daughter of a railroad man, described her father's horror at the very idea of the railroad hiring her. He told her, "'You can't do it. You're not strong enough to do it. You just don't understand. It's a man's job.'"

Above all, "He was scared to death every day. I was gonna do something wrong to disgrace him."[133] She also remembered terrible racism, with the men she worked with telling her, "We don't like you. But you're better than—I'll never say the word. That was one of the things we were told on a daily basis. You don't belong here, but you're better than, you can imagine the word that was used."

Most would have liked to keep their jobs but were quickly let go once the war had ended. "I think we were always intruders. They got rid of us the minute they could." That was the deal with war jobs: "The war was over, it was time to go back to doing the dishes."[134]

GLORIA RICHARDSON

Civil Rights Leader
Cambridge, Maryland, USA
1963

Fight for what you believe in, but stop being so nice. [135]
— Gloria Richardson

In 1963 the governor of Maryland declared martial law to quell civil rights demonstrations. Richardson, a local movement leader, was talking to the men on the street here when she was rudely interrupted by a National Guardsman and his bayonet. Her aplomb, while pushing the bayonet away, is magnificent. "I wasn't afraid," Richardson later recalled. "I was upset. And if I was upset enough, I didn't have time to be afraid. And besides, we had guns, too." [136]

Two years before, she was a divorced mother of two, a graduate of Howard University who was living back in her hometown of Cambridge, where Black unemployment was at thirty percent. Her father was the town pharmacist, and she was working in his store when she stepped up to lead the local affiliate of the Student Nonviolent Coordinating Committee.

Cambridge was a small town but only 90 miles (145 kilometers) from Washington, D.C. The actions there came to be known as the Cambridge Movement, and national leaders got involved in negotiating a settlement to the continuing protests. Attorney General Robert Kennedy, the president's brother, pushed for the town to vote on what was called the Treaty of Cambridge. Richardson refused his whole idea: "A first-class citizen does not plead to the white power structure to give him something that the whites have no power to give or take away. Human rights are human rights, not white rights." [137] Kennedy invited her to a White House meeting—where he asked her if she knew how to smile. "We were there to talk about civil rights. That was nothing to smile about," Richardson later said. [138]

At the legendary March on Washington a month later, Diane Nash was the only woman to speak, for one minute. Richardson was also scheduled to address the huge crowd, but as soon as she was handed the microphone and said, "Hello," a NAACP official snatched the mic away. Decades later, she said she was cut off because she "hadn't dressed up properly, and was a woman, and a series of things." [139] That "series of things" presumably references her radicalism, which put her at odds with some, but meanwhile the leadership at the march was "totally men," which gave an inaccurate representation of the movement. [140]

Richardson lived long enough to see the Black Lives Matter movement sweep the country. "This goes on and on," she warned in 2020. "We marched until the governor called martial law. That's when you get their attention. Otherwise, you're going to keep protesting the same things another 100 years from now." [141]

LAKSHMI SAHGAL

Doctor and Freedom Fighter
Singapore
1940

Sahgal, who was born a rich girl in Madras, India, made one of her first decisions to rebel when she took the hand of a tribal girl in open defiance of her grandmother, who described such people, some of her fellow human beings, as those "whose very shadows are polluting." [142]

Sahgal became a doctor and then an ardent fighter for Indian independence, recruiting and leading the Rani of Jhansi Regiment, an all-woman fighting force, and even recording the army song "Chalo Dilli" (On to Delhi!) In this photograph, she is standing to the right of her inspiration and leader, Subhas Chandra Bose, who was a complicated figure. He was an important anticolonialist nationalist, an enemy of the British occupiers of India, who ended up allying himself with the Axis powers during World War II—mostly due to the old idea that the enemy of my enemy is my friend.

Sahgal's extraordinary women's army, and Bose's efforts to invade India from Burma in the east with the help of the Japanese government, failed quite miserably, but they both remain nationalist heroes. He died in a 1945 plane crash, but she lived to be ninety-seven and became almost a symbol of Indian independence.

Known after the war years as "Captain Lakshmi," in civilian life she was a devoted doctor for decades. She was in Calcutta in 1971, treating wounded refugees from the division of Bangladesh; in 1984 she went to treat the victims of the Bhopal factory explosion. She was a leftist activist and even ran for president of India at eighty-seven—failing by far, as she expected—and she remained a beloved inspiration to a great many until her death in 2012.

ESTHER MCCREADY

Nurse
Baltimore, Maryland, USA
1950

The only woman here was a star student whose application to the public University of Maryland School of Nursing was rejected because she was Black. Standing to her left is a young Thurgood Marshall, who successfully argued McCready's case against the university. Marshall went on to become one of the greatest ever American lawyers and a justice on the US Supreme Court.

The other men are distinguished lawyers from the National Association for the Advancement of Colored People and their clients, whose law suits each pushed open the university's schools of medicine, engineering, sociology, and pharmacy to Black people. Together these are the people who accomplished the legal desegregation of the University of Maryland, case by painstaking case, in the years before public school segregation by law were declared unconstitutional in 1954.

McCready lost her case at first but was successful on appeal. However, as other stories in this book also show, winning admission to public life is not the end of the fight. "The decision was handed down that the university had to admit me, and that was another song and dance. It was such an experience," McCready said, with a laugh in 2012. [143] When finally studying at the school, she faced all kinds of hostility from faculty and students who refused to live or eat with her.

After graduating in 1953, McCready worked as a nurse in several locations, including the emergency room of New York's Harlem Hospital, and taught in New York public schools. She was also a classically trained singer who earned degrees from the Manhattan School of Music, toured Europe and the United States, and sang in the Metropolitan Opera chorus.

UNKNOWN

Nurse
Boston, Massachusetts, USA
1890

We know where this photo was taken: Boston City Hospital, one of thousands of public hospitals founded in the wake of the Civil War. Operating theaters like this one were popular teaching spaces that offered real drama while fluffing the fame and prestige of the star surgeons. We know the identity of the photographer and the stars in this play: the surgeon Herbert L. Burrell of Harvard Medical School stands to the right, and a Dr. Cheever is operating on the leg of this unfortunate, who is at least inhaling ether. But the nurse? Her identity is unknown, probably forever lost. Nevertheless, she is playing an important role. Like an angel, in white, she is there to comfort the patient, support the doctors, and dazzle the spectators. Her presence seems to sanctify the painful scene.

At the time of this photograph, nurses were struggling to establish decent professional standards; many were treated as servants by hospitals that expected them to work around the clock, devoting themselves body and soul like nuns, for no or little pay.

Florence Nightingale, the English nursing pioneer, declared, "Every woman is a nurse."[144]

She meant that in private life, most women will be called upon to take care of someone—be it baby, parent, or spouse—and that universality was a basis upon which to build a new profession for women. Even today, in the US and Canada, almost ninety percent of registered nurses are women.

Nursing is obviously closely identified with women, and is the clearest example of how traditionally female jobs are often associated with our bodies: the very word comes from nursing: breastfeeding a child. Often, the Only Women pictured in this book are doing a woman's job. Playing one of the roles specially designated for women can provide an entrée into an otherwise all-male space.

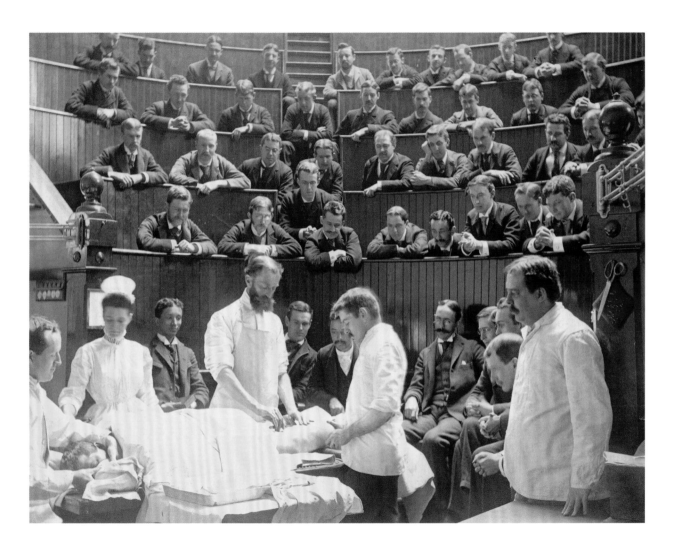

ÁNGELA RAMOS

Journalist
Ate-Vitarte, Peru
1929

The battle for the feminine is just about to begin. [145]
—Ángela Ramos, 1988

Nicknamed Sor Presa (Sister of the Imprisoned), Ramos is often described as the first Peruvian woman journalist. Her articles were weapons in her lifelong crusade to help the oppressed, especially the imprisoned, cheated workers, and victims of harsh vagrancy laws, which the police used to sweep up poor people and put them into forced labor. In her columns, she denounced prisons full of "rotting men" and called the vagrancy law "a horrible felony, since it reduces man to the condition of a slave, of a human beast, since he is forced into labor, not paid even the slightest salary, and his naked body is whipped." [146]

She wrote with the passion of experience: her very first article was an enraged complaint on her own behalf. The wage cheating that she felt killed her father had also happened to her, after working for years at an English steamship company, and she wasn't having it. She was a feminist and suffragist, and a sympathizer with the communism of José Carlos Mariátegui, the influential activist, who is sitting just behind her in the car, wearing glasses. They were attending the annual Fiesta de la Planta in the Peruvian factory town of Vitarte (now Ate-Vitarte), where workers had won the eight-hour day. *La planta* referred to both living and industrial plants; the festival concluded with a massive tree planting.

Ramos also wrote a screenplay! A director who had just made the first feature in Bolivia approached her, and together they created the film *El carnaval del amor* (*The Carnival of Love*) (1930), a well-received melodrama— with progressive twists.

UNKNOWN

Communist
Moscow, Russia
1922

Most of the men gathered here are unidentified Communists, gathered from around the world as delegates and other participants in the 4th World Congress of the Communist International, or Comintern. It is notable how comfortable and intimate they seem to feel, including the only woman, who is tucked in right in the middle.

A few faces jump out, including the two ill-fated cozy fellows up front, Nikolai Bukharin, political theorist, economist, and newspaper editor, leaning on Grigory Zinoviev, then chairman of the Communist International. Both would be executed. Also easy to spot, in the second row left, is the Jamaican-American poet Claude McKay, who came on his own impetus and addressed the congress on the relationship of Black people, specifically African Americans, to the international Communist movement. The congress

was almost but not entirely a male proceeding. Among the crowd of delegates, women were scattered here and there, including a handful of prominent women leaders, such as the German revolutionary Clara Zetkin, who gave an address on "The Woman Question," i.e. the relationship of women to the international Communist movement.

Historian Maurice Casey, who specializes in international revolutionaries and unearthed the photo in 2019 in a personal archive in California, suspects that the only woman here "is one of the many Comintern stenographers and translators, disproportionately women, who have entirely slipped into obscurity." [147] He is working to unearth their stories, and has found at least three who came to Moscow from London's East End, where they had been militant workers in the movement for women's suffrage.

ELISA MCINROY

Revolutionary
Chicago, Illinois, USA
1969

McInroy was an education major at the University of Iowa and a supporter of the liberal presidential candidate Eugene McCarthy when she signed up to be a volunteer teacher in Chicago for the summer of 1968. She took a Greyhound bus and used the one phone number a friend had given her and immediately ended up in a political meeting in a radical bookstore.

Many Americans were radicalized by witnessing Chicago in the summer of 1968 on their TV screens, seeing police brutality in real time—but for those who lived it, it was an intense initiation into revolutionary politics. When McInroy went back to college after that summer, she "could not relate to anything after being tear gassed every night during the convention, it was just too much of a culture shock." She ended up back in Chicago, teaching in a progressive elementary school and co-founding a newspaper called *Rising Up Angry*. She also did feminist work and learned to be an abortion counselor.

In a conversation in 2021, she recalled, "The Black Panthers were organizing Black street gangs, and we were organizing white street kids, trying to convince them not to kill each other but to fight the real enemy, the police." The work McInroy and her comrades did would come to fruition in the first Rainbow Coalition, a legendary, if short-lived, model for the American left.

This press conference, held on the first anniversary of Martin Luther King Jr.'s assassination, included representatives from the Black Panther Party, the Young Lords (the Puerto Rican revolutionary group), and radicalized whites from the Young Patriots, Rise Up Angry (RUA), and Jobs or Income Now (JOIN).

McInroy, age twenty-one, is standing next to her comrade and future lifelong husband Jim Cartier. They are barely visible behind the much taller Bobby Rush, the Black Panther Party member and future congressman, and Alfredo Matias of the Young Lords. The image has become iconic, but in all the times that it has been used and the men ID'd in captions, Elisa McInroy has scarcely been mentioned. Of the photo, she said, "I liked being with all those men. I like men too." [148]

Seated L–R: JACK "JUNEBUG" BOYKIN, HENRY "POISON" GADDIS, NATHANIEL JUNIOR, and LUIS CUZO.

Standing L–R: ANDY KENISTON, HY THURMAN, WILLIAM FESPERMAN, BOBBY MCGINNIS, MICHAEL JAMES, BUD PAULIN, BOBBY RUSH, JIM CARTIER, ELISA MCINROY and ALFREDO MATIAS

SHIRLEY CLARKE

Filmmaker
New York, New York, USA
c. 1962

In this photo, notable filmmakers and wannabes form a ring around the heart of things: Clarke, passionate friend and radical filmmaker, avatar of hip, embodiment of the spirit of New York, the Chelsea Hotel, and jazz. Clarke was often described as "the only woman" in this generation of New York filmmakers who invented American independent film, and in the intertwined cinema verité documentary movement. Members of the New American Cinema Group (later known as the American New Wave) did not share any style but rather were united in a belief in personal, noncorporate, anti-Hollywood filmmaking. They worked to create cinema as a personal independent art in the United States, as it was in Japan and Europe and elsewhere on the postwar globe.

Clarke was never, in fact, literally the only woman: there were others making films, and they were friends, collaborators, employees. For example for her second feature (*The Cool World*, 1964), she hired the first Black female documentary filmmaker, Madeline Anderson, to work with her on the set and in the edit room. But there is a phenomenon of cultural spotlighting: a narrow shaft of light picking out a single woman so that she is the only one seen. She becomes the Only Woman in the public eye and memory. Looking back in 1983, Clarke described a global phenomenon in the 1960s: "Each country was allowed one female filmmaker. You know, like Varda in France and Wertmüller in Italy, Chytilová in Czechoslovakia, Mai Zetterling in Sweden, and Shirley Clarke in the United States. It was tokenism. But at the same time I became famous because I was the token. You know, when you're the only one, that helps also. So that's lucky. It's dumb and it's sad and it's pathetic but I didn't have competition."[149]

Slowly, she felt less amused by that status and dropped film for early video art making. Just as she had advocated for more Black filmmakers, so she did too for more women. And she felt discouraged by shadowboxing with sexism; she knew that her male counterparts had a very different time of it over their careers. "Had you been a man, your career would have been a hundred times better, you would not have had the problems you had, you would not have been thought of as this batty lady, but a great artist."[150]

Clockwise from top: ED BLAND, UNIDENTIFIED, RICKY LEACOCK, UNIDENTIFIED, GREGORY MARKOUPOULOS, STAN BRAKHAGE, and H. L. "DOC" HUMES.

Center: <u>SHIRLEY CLARKE</u>

PAM HOGG

Designer
London, England, UK
1992

The photographer wanted to take her picture, so she asked him how he wanted to take her. But then she told him she wanted to pose with one hundred naked men. Right, he said, brilliant. [151]

So, these eleven chaps are the stalwart tenth, the friends and exes, volunteer models. She said that they were actually quite shy in the moment, and they seem very sweet indeed. Quite serious though—how did they manage that?

Hogg is in her rightful place, in the middle and ruling. An art school grad from Glasgow, she was a painter and musician who came up through the club scene in punk, postpunk, and New Romantic London. She says that she fell into designing clothes because she and her friends were so terrified of not meeting favor with the all-powerful door people at clubs that they inspired each other into a creative frenzy of creating the best outfits, looks that would guarantee entry and envy—and joy. And she just never ever stopped.

Well, in fact, she did stop, because she hasn't yet figured out how to make enough money to make the work sustainable. Instead, she was always working like an old-style artist, too much on her own and with too little cash and support. But she always came back. In 2014 she was lured back from one hiatus when she was asked to help honor Pussy Riot, the radical Russian protest performers and punk band, and she just could not say no, and then she was hooked again. She can name drop with the best of them—she has played with her friend Debbie Harry and made clothes for Rihanna, Kylie, Alison Mosshart, and Siouxsie Sioux.

She favors catsuits, of every kind, and promises that once you've gone cat, you'll be a changed person. Other than that, she has gone through so many collections that she's done something of almost everything, except, of course, for square; she is interested in plastics, rubbers, color riots, shine, sparkle, and spirit. Her sensibility always shines through; the clothes are full of warmth and humor, freedom, play, and beauty.

Model
Paris, France
c. 1900

This photograph could be titled *Ceci n'est pas une poire*, *Frenchmen at Work*, or *The History of Western Art*. Or perhaps the artists in this studio are self-aware feminists who are sending up centuries of sexist artistic convention. Unlikely, but it would be pretty cool.

Here the European men have faces, names, careers—and clothes—while the woman lies facelessly at their feet. She is the Only and the Other, the not-quite-human object of study, like the skeleton who echoes her reclining odalisque pose. She embodies the familiar paradoxes of women in patriarchy: she is beauty, close to divinity, a powerful object of adoration; she is a prisoner and as close to the devil as to god.

Modeling as a profession emerged in nineteenth-century painters' studios, as a woman's job. Her work is to be an object, usually of beauty, but also to inspire, even to become a muse. But who were they in real life? A life model was usually a working-class woman who fell into one of the three named types studios advertised for: Italian, Jew, or *Parisienne*. Historians are seeking to learn more about the flesh-and-blood people, who often turned to modeling as a way station either into or out of sex work. They were women who were managing to commodify their beauty, turning it into a source of power or a means of survival.

MARY "MAY" MORRIS

Designer
London, England, UK
1893

Morris is pictured here with the staff of the Kelmscott Press, next to her father, William Morris, the great polymath of the British Arts and Crafts Movement. An artist, designer, writer, and printer, William was also an activist who, despite his wealthy origins, helped win acceptance of socialism in *fin de siècle* Britain.

May, as multitalented as her father—she wrote plays and poetry, in addition to her activism and groundbreaking work in design—stepped into the family business. At twenty-three, she took over the embroidery department of Morris & Co., becoming responsible for producing a stream of new patterns and designs for wallpapers and fabrics, in addition to supervising a team of embroiderers, although credit for her designs was given to William, "in the interests of commercial success."[152]

May's mother, Jane Burden, was the daughter of a stableman and a laundress, but one night at the theater she caught the eye of Dante Gabriel Rossetti and Edward Burne-Jones, who, struck by her beauty, asked her to model for them. Burden also sat for William, who, naturally, fell in love with her. Although by her own admission, she was not in love with William, she married him and reinvented herself in the role of gentleman's wife. She had no trouble moving in upper-class circles and may have inspired George Bernard Shaw, a family friend, in his creation of the character Eliza Doolittle.

Like a Pre-Raphaelite version of the family depicted in the film *The Royal Tenenbaums*, themselves a postmodern version of J. D. Salinger's Glass family, the Morrises were evidence that all unconventional families are alike: superficially eccentric but ultimately hamstrung by society—and their hearts. May and her sister, Jenny, were the flowers of this hothouse milieu, gallivanting about in loose "artistic dresses" and climbing trees. "I am a great tomboy," an eight-year-old May wrote in her journal.[153] That did not inoculate her, years later, against a crush on George Bernard Shaw. Shaw, alas, was still living at home and involved with a much older woman.

Morris's approach to embroidery was innovative, and influential. "May helped elevate embroidery to an art form," says Rowan Bain, senior curator at the William Morris Gallery in London.[154] After her father's death, she had a successful career as a designer, maker, and exhibitor. She had a lifelong commitment to socialism and feminism, and in the face of women's exclusion from all existing guilds, founded the Women's Guild of Arts in 1907. She also dedicated almost ten years to editing the twenty-four volumes of her father's *Collected Works*. Her own extraordinary accomplishments have always been overshadowed by his. In 1936 Morris wrote in a letter to George Bernard Shaw. "I'm a remarkable woman," she wrote, "always was, though none of you seemed to think so."[155]

Wm Morris. May Morris

BENAZIR BHUTTO

Politician
Pakistan
1988

"She has run as her father's daughter, more a Bhutto than a woman," explained the *New York Times* when Benazir Bhutto, at the age of thirty-five, the day this photo was taken in 1988, was elected the world's youngest Prime Minister and the first woman Prime Minister of a Muslim-majority country. [156]

Her image here sums up her electric appeal—fearlessly plunging into all-male rough and tumble, while projecting an almost holy calm and piety—and perhaps revealing the brilliance of Salman Rushdie's snarky name for a character based on her: *Virgin Ironpants.*

The daughter of a rich aristocratic family, educated at Harvard and Oxford, she was only twenty-four when her Prime Minister father was ousted in a military coup and then, two years later, executed by hanging. She took his place as party leader and vowed to avenge him. As leader of the opposition she was arrested, imprisoned, placed in solitary confinement, and under house arrest, more times than you can count.

Finally, General Zia, her arch-nemesis who overthrew her father, died in a mysterious plane crash. The C-130, returning from a demonstration of American tanks in the desert, went down with the US ambassador and four of Pakistan's five top generals, Three months later, Bhutto was elected. She had recently agreed to an arranged marriage and given birth to her first child; she called the crash an act of god.

Nothing got any easier—or less dramatic. While the nation faced severe difficulties, she had a first not very distinguished term of two years, then more years in opposition and exile, and a comeback second term in the 1990s. When police killed her rivalrous brother, some—including, for a while, her own mother—accused her of being involved with his death. But only a few weeks after her brother's killing, she herself was deposed by the military. She was also accused, much more credibly, of impressive corruption.

In 2007, after another eight years in exile, she was brave enough to return for yet another comeback campaign. Right away her welcome home was marked by a bombing—150 people died but she survived. In the words of the journalist Amy Wilentz, who knew her personally and professionally, "as her father's daughter, she couldn't obey the ineluctable logic of the new Pakistan: wouldn't stay inside, wouldn't shun the people, wouldn't go back into exile after the first attack." [157]

Only two months later, in a tragic scene not unlike this photo, she was waving to a cheering crowd when she was killed by a suicide bomber.

LÉA LINSTER

Chef
Collonges-au-Mont-d'Or, France
2016

Léa Linster is from Luxembourg, whose traditional cuisine is plenty mouth-watering what with dumplings, Rhine wine, fresh perch, and a great intimacy with the way of the potato. She remembers the first meal she made for guests at the age of 16: chicken in a Riesling sauce and a plum tart.

Her family ran a road stop with a gas station, bistro, bowling alley, and *tabac*. When her father died young, she took over the family business and eventually made that bistro into a thing of splendor. After she won her first Michelin star in 1989, she was tapped to represent Luxembourg at a two-year-old international cooking competition, the Bocuse d'Or, named for the super chef Paul Bocuse himself, who dreamt it up with his showman's instinct. She laid her roast lamb in a potato crust on big Paul—and he laid on her the golden miniature of himself, now the most hyped prize in cuisine.

Bocuse, the first fully branded celebrity chef, had a schtick that was almost like a parody of "the Frenchman" from back in the day: the man in a towering phallic toque, a lover of women, wine, and food in equal measure. He was a generous, arrogant bon vivant—and a notorious enemy of women in cuisine. He would make statements like, "I would rather have a pretty woman in my bed than behind a stove in a restaurant." [158]

When he turned ninety in 2016, all the winners of the Bocuse d'Or gathered around him at his restaurant near Lyon. Linster was the only woman. What do you get a man who has everything, including a wife and two lovers, immense fame, and one of the greatest restaurants in the world? The assembled winners bought him a statue of himself, a copy of the original in the city center.

Linster has been a warm defender of Bocuse, whom she clearly loved like a father. Her reign as the first-and-only woman top prize winner is even longer than film director Jane Campion's twenty-eight years with Cannes' Palme d'Or and film director Kathryn Bigelow's puny twelve with a Best Director Oscar—for Linster, it's been thirty-two years and counting, as of 2021. But it's a distinction she is not happy about. She says she has only one regret about her career, which is "that there aren't more female candidates in the Bocuse d'Or!" [159]

MARY PICKFORD

Actor and Film Producer
Los Angeles, California, USA
1919

Abandoned by her father, Pickford was an impoverished child in Canada, who began performing at an early age from urgent need. "I'm the father of my family and I've got to earn all the money I can." [160] She quickly moved from the stage to the newfangled screen. She relocated to Hollywood, California, in 1916 when she was twenty-five, becoming one of the first, biggest, and richest stars, seemingly doubling her salary every two years as she hopscotched between studios, scoring hits for each. She was referred to as "America's Sweetheart" and the "Queen of the Movies."

Pickford and fellow megastars Douglas Fairbanks, D. W. Griffith, and Charlie Chaplin—they were known as the Big Four—are pictured here in 1919 at the creation of their own production company, United Artists. This was a revolutionary move in the film business—actors and directors had never owned their own companies before. Their risk paid off. They succeeded in controlling their own work instead of working for studio bosses.

Women were numerous and powerful in the early years of movie making. Hollywood was lousy with women producers, directors, screenwriters, editors, stars, and studio owners in the silent era. This fact was long obscured by many subsequent decades of male dominance, but recent efforts to excavate the truth are succeeding; word is spreading that women once held the reins.

Although one can find many photos of Pickford in which she is the only woman, film historian Cari Beauchamp stresses that Pickford in fact often worked with other women, including her best friend, Frances Marion, the fabulously successful and prolific screenwriter. [161] Marion had regular all-women parties, which helped cement the important network of female friendships that made the business run.

It was the advent of sound that changed things. Costs tripled, drawing new Wall Street investment and transforming movie production into an industry. "Men muscled into high-paying positions," Beauchamp writes, "and women were sidelined to the point where, by the 1950s, speakers at Directors Guild meetings began their comments with 'Gentlemen and Miss Lupino,' as Ida Lupino was their only female member." [162]

NINALEE CRAIG

Art Student
Florence, Italy
1951

Ruth Orkin, the photographer of this iconic picture, had a lot in common with her subject, Craig. They were both twenty-three-year-old American artists who were traveling and exploring the world on their own. They met by chance and agreed to spend a couple of days together having fun and taking pictures to document Craig's daily life. *American Girl in Italy* was in that portfolio, created before Orkin made her name as a photographer and filmmaker.

Orkin had been taking pictures since age ten, and by twelve was using her own darkroom at home in Los Angeles. At seventeen she wanted to visit the 1939 New York World's Fair, so she took a four-month summer bicycle trip across the country—alone.

Many viewers nowadays detect more than a whiff of menace in the image; what feels like sport or even homage to men can be menacing and infuriating street harassment to women. Just being the Only Woman on the street can feel—and be—dangerous.

However, both Orkin and Craig saw this photo as a celebration of their own female independence and freedom. At age eighty-seven, Craig explained:

"It was a very difficult time, just after the war, and men of all ages were hanging around the city centre. And I was admired, but personally I don't see anything wrong with an appreciative whistle. You can tell I was from another country and, being 6 ft, I was an object of curiosity. They were just showing their appreciation. Oh, and that poor soul touching himself? I was used to it. It was almost like a good luck sign for the Italian man, making sure the family jewels were intact. When it was first published, that was occasionally airbrushed out but I would never consider it to be a vulgar gesture. My expression is not one of distress, that was just how I stalked around the city. I saw myself as Beatrice of Dante's Divine Comedy. You had to walk with complete assurance and maintain a dignity at all times ... This image has been interpreted in a sinister way but it was quite the opposite. They were having fun and so was I."[163]

MARLENE DIETRICH

Star
European Front
1945

Dietrich, an all-time great female star, was the very "symbol of glamour," according to the headline of her obituary in the *New York Times* in 1992. She is famous for her trademark seductive play with masculine and feminine appeal. Here, she is working for the US Army, entertaining soldiers in Europe during the war. A devoted anti-Fascist, Dietrich was horrified by what her native Germany had turned into, and she did wartime service by donating her femininity, her glamour, and her fame, visiting soldiers to encourage them and cheer them up. In that role, she embodied a mix of archetypal Only Woman categories: nurse, sex worker, and angel!

Becoming a performer—dancer, singer, actor—has long been a pathway for a woman to enter public life. Becoming a *star* has been a rare chance for a woman to gain real money and power. Showbiz has had many Only Women, who managed to enter and shine, very often one at a time, in a male fantasy on-screen and off.

Although they are still fewer in number than men and are paid less, we are so used to women stars now that it's easy to forget how off-limits public performance once was. Historically, women made a long and slow climb onto the stage: societies went to lengths to keep them off stage, unseen and unheard in public. All the great women's roles in classical theater and Shakespeare, played by boy actors. And imagine actually *castrating boys* to get soprano voices without women.

IESHIA EVANS

Revolutionary
Baton Rouge, Louisiana, USA
2016

I think I will be remembered as a peaceful protester who saw injustice going on and took a stand. I'd like to be remembered as a revolutionary. [164]
—Ieshia Evans

In 2016 police in Baton Rouge, Louisiana, shot and killed Alton Sterling in yet another outrageous horror killing of an innocent Black American. In the protests that responded was Evans, a nurse who had come down from Pennsylvania expressly to be there in solidarity.

Taking a Stand in Baton Rouge, as this photograph is known, captures the fleeting moment before the cops grabbed Evans and detained her for twenty-four hours in the county jail. Her poise and her position as the sole woman create the power of the photo, which is so much about contrast: one versus many, female versus male, Black versus white, vulnerable and flowy versus hard shelled and robotic, right versus wrong, peace versus violence. She joins a noble tradition of courageous sole women and men standing up against state power, such as the Tank Man in Tiananmen Square in 1989 and the girl with a flower at the Pentagon in 1967.

The image become so famous that Evans was asked to re-enact it for a spread in Harper's Bazaar. To Evans, the photo is about the movement and not her own image. As she told the BBC— "I do like the photo. There's feminine power there, there's Black power there." [165]

However, she also stressed that its message is not all lovey-dovey. "People of good conscience, people with a good heart—like some people back in the '60s. When they were risking their lives, it wasn't just them standing in protest. It wasn't something like what I did, standing in front of police officers. Even though that's dangerous, there are more worthwhile efforts, like uncovering the truth about what's really going on." [166]

TIMELINE 220

**MRS. FAIRFAX
COOK**
Harrison's Landing, Virginia, USA
1862

**UNKNOWN
NURSE**
Boston, Massachusetts, USA
1890

**UNKNOWN
MASCOT**
Annapolis, Maryland, USA
1894

**UNKNOWN
STUDENT**
Nashville, Tennessee, USA
1899

**ANNA FRANSEN LA MONTAGNE
GOLDMINER**
Fairbanks, Alaska, USA
c. 1900

**SOPHIE MOSSEAU
UNKNOWN**
Fort Laramie, Wyoming, USA
c. 1868–70

**MARY "MAY" MORRIS
DESIGNER**
London, England, UK
1893

**ANNA SEARCY
MEDICAL STUDENT**
Columbia, Missouri, USA
1897

**ELLEN SWALLOW RICHARDS
ENVIRONMENTAL CHEMIST**
Cambridge, Massachusetts, USA
1900

**UNKNOWN
MODEL**
Paris, France
c. 1900

1910s

UNKNOWN
MODEL
Paris, France
c. 1900

ETHEL BENJAMIN
LAWYER
Dunedin, New Zealand
1902

LAUFEY VALDIMARSDÓTTIR
SCHOOL STUDENT
Reykjavik, Iceland
1910

EMMELINE PANKHURST
SUFFRAGETTE
London, England, UK
1914

KOMAKO KIMURA
PERFORMING ARTIST
New York, New York, USA
1917

UNKNOWN
COWGIRL
Unknown, USA
c. 1900

CIXI
EMPRESS
Beijing, China
c. 1903

MARIE CURIE
PHYCISIST AND CHEMIST
Brussels, Belgium
1911

JOVITA IDÁR
JOURNALIST AND ACTIVIST
Laredo, Texas, USA
1914

UNKNOWN
SHIPYARD WORKER
Aberdeen, Washington, USA
1918

MARY PICKFORD
ACTOR AND FILM PRODUCER
Los Angeles, California, USA
1919

BESSIE SMITH
JAZZ MUSICIAN
Philadelphia, Pennsylvania, USA
c. 1920

MADELINE LINFORD
NEWSPAPER EDITOR
Manchester, England, UK
1921

FLORENCE NORTH
BOXING PROMOTER
New York, New York, USA
1922

LIL HARDIN
MUSICIAN AND SONGWRITER
Chicago, Illinois, USA
1923

JESSIE BOYD SCRIVER
MEDICAL STUDENT
Montreal, Canada
1920

GERTRUDE BELL
IMPERIALIST
Cairo, Egypt
1921

ANNA DE NOAILLES
POET
Paris, France
1922

UNKNOWN
COMMUNIST
Moscow, Russia
1922

LATIFE HANIM
WIFE
Turkey
1923

SIMONE KAHN BRETON
GALLERIST
Paris, France
1924

CLARA A. PRATT
BOTANIST
Niagara Glen, Canada
1924

MABEL GRIFFITH
POLICE OFFICER
Anaheim, California, USA
1927

ÁNGELA RAMOS
JOURNALIST
Ate-Vitarte, Peru
1929

ANNA HELLER ROZENTAL
BUNDIST
Vienna, Austria
1931

MARGARET NAYLOR
DIVER
Tobermory Bay, Scotland, UK
1924

GUNTA STÖLZL
TEXTILE ARTIST
Dessau, Germany
1926

VERA MENCHIK
CHESS CHAMPION
Karlovy Vary, Czechoslovakia
1929

FRIDA KAHLO
ARTIST
Mexico City, Mexico
1929

VIRGINIA WRIGHT
STICK-UP ARTIST
New York, New York, USA
1931

1930s

1940s

GERTRUDE TREVELYAN
WRITER
Oxford, England, UK
1933

ELLEN WILKINSON
POLITICIAN
Harrogate, England, UK
1936

DOROTHY PARKER
WRITER
New York, New York, USA
1938

FRANCES PERKINS
POLITICIAN
Washington, D.C., USA
c. 1939

UNKNOWN
RAILROAD WORKER
Pennsylvania, USA
c.1942–44

COLETTE
WRITER
Paris, France
1936

THYRA EDWARDS
ACTIVIST AND EDUCATOR
Washington, D.C., USA
1937

CHRISTINA BROOM
PHOTOGRAPHER
Oxford, England, UK
1938

LAKSHMI SAHGAL
DOCTOR AND
FREEDOM FIGHTER
Singapore
1940

MARTHA GELLHORN
WAR CORRESPONDENT
Cassino, Italy
1944

MARLENE DIETRICH
STAR
European Front
1945

ALICE CHALIFOUX
HARPIST
Cleveland, Ohio, USA
1946

ELIZABETH ROBOZ EINSTEIN
BIOCHEMIST
Denver, Colorado, USA
1946

MARION CARPENTER
PHOTOGRAPHER
Washington, D.C., USA
1947

ELAINE DE KOONING
PAINTER
Black Mountain, North Carolina, USA
1948

AMY GERALDINE "DINAH" STOCK
ANTI-IMPERIALIST
Manchester, England, UK
c. 1945

LEONA WOODS
PHYSICIST
Chicago, Illinois, USA
1946

ETHEL STARK
VIOLINIST AND CONDUCTOR
Montreal, Canada
c. 1946

GRACIELA
SINGER
New York, New York, USA
1947

ESTHER MCCREADY
NURSE
Baltimore, Maryland, USA
1950

HEDDA STERNE
ARTIST
New York, New York, USA
1951

LISETTE DAMMAS
JUROR
New York, New York, USA
1951

LUCILLE KALLEN
TELEVISION COMEDY WRITER
New York, New York, USA
1952

ABIGAIL HOFFMAN
HOCKEY PLAYER
Toronto, Canada
1956

ETHEL "SUNNY" LOWRY
SWIMMER
Folkestone, England, UK
1960

NINALEE CRAIG
ART STUDENT
Florence, Italy
1951

KATHERINE HOWARD
POLITICIAN
Chicago, Illinois, USA
1952

CHRISTINE JORGENSEN
ENTERTAINER AND TRANS
RIGHTS ADVOCATE
New York, New York, USA
1953

NATHALIE SARRAUTE
WRITER
Paris, France
1959

CLARISSA WIMBUSH
DENTIST
Alexandria, Virginia, USA
1961

SHIRLEY CLARKE
FILMMAKER
New York, New York, USA
c. 1962

GLORIA RICHARDSON
CIVIL RIGHTS LEADER
Cambridge, Maryland, USA
1963

STELLA LEVY
EDITORIAL ASSISTANT
San Francisco, California, USA
1965

NINA SCHULMAN
FILMMAKER
Monterey, California, USA
1967

ELISA MCINROY
REVOLUTIONARY
Chicago, Illinois, USA
1969

VALENTINA TERESHKOVA
COSMONAUT
Former USSR
1963

UNKNOWN
SECRETARY
London, England, UK
1964

KATHRINE SWITZER
ATHLETE
Boston, Massachusetts, USA
1967

JOANN MORGAN
SPACE ENGINEER
Cape Canaveral, Florida, USA
1969

LUCY KOMISAR
ACTIVIST AND JOURNALIST
New York, New York, USA
1970

SHIRLEY CHISHOLM
POLITICIAN
New York, New York, USA
1972

BETSY WADE
NEWSPAPER EDITOR
New York, New York, USA
1975

JANET GUTHRIE
RACE CAR DRIVER
Trenton, New Jersey, USA
1976

DIANA SPENCER
TEACHING ASSISTANT
London, England, UK
1980

MIA WESTERLUND ROOSEN
SCULPTOR
New York, New York, USA
1982

MING SMITH
PHOTOGRAPHER
New York, New York, USA
1973

KATHARINE GRAHAM
PUBLISHER
New York, New York, USA
1975

MARGARET THATCHER
POLITICIAN
London, England, UK
1979

ANDREA MOTLEY CRABTREE
US ARMY DEEP SEA DIVER
Panama City, Florida, USA
1982

RITA LEVI-MONTALCINI
NEUROBIOLOGIST
Vatican City, Italy
1986

| 1990s | 2000s | 2010s | 2020s |

ELIZABETH BARTHOLET
LAW PROFESSOR
Cambridge, Massachusetts, USA
1987

BENAZIR BHUTTO
POLITICIAN
Pakistan
1988

JANE CAMPION
FILMMAKER
Cannes, France
2007

IESHIA EVANS
REVOLUTIONARY
Baton Rouge, Louisiana, USA
2016

CHRISTINE LAGARDE
INTERNATIONAL BANKER
Fukuoka, Japan
2019

BONNIE DUNBAR
ASTRONAUT
Mir Space Station
1988

PAM HOGG
DESIGNER
London, England, UK
1992

LÉA LINSTER
CHEF
Collonges-au-Mont-d'Or, France
2016

SATSUKI KATAYAMA
POLITICIAN
Tokyo, Japan
2018

SARAH FULLER
FOOTBALL PLAYER
Nashville, Tennessee, USA
2020

End notes

01 From the article "More Confessions of a Sensualist," by Gael Greene published in *New York Magazine*, January 28, 1974.

02 From her speech at Variety's Power of Women luncheon, as reported in "Tina Fey Wants You to Know That Women Are Not 'Cappuccino Machines'" by Anna Silman in *The Cut*, April 13, 2018.

03 The original essay, "The Smurfette Principle," by Katha Pollitt, was published in the *New York Times Magazine*, April 7, 1991. It has engendered a wealth of continuing commentary since its publication. For examples, see its Wikipedia page and this 2011 video with clips, by Anita Sarkeesian feministfrequency.com/video/tropes-vs-women-3-the-smurfette-principle.

04 Dr. Garrett generously shared her research with the author, in a telephone conversation and also in the text of her 2019 talk, "Women in Medicine at Mizzou."

05 Writer Sarah Boxer interviewed Hedda Sterne in 2003, and draws on their exchange in "The Last Irascible," her astute and moving appreciation of Sterne published in *The New York Review of Books*, not long after Sterne's death in 2010.

06 Curator Sarah Eckhardt, an authority on, and a close friend of, Sterne's, cited this remark in her essay for the catalog of the exhibition she curated, "Uninterrupted Flux."

07 Art historian and curator Phyllis Tuchman conducted an interview with Hedda Sterne in 1981 for the Archives of American Art at the Smithsonian Institution. The interview was about Mark Rothko but, apparently intuitively, Tuchman knew to digress and ask Sterne how she felt about the 1951 photo.

08 Also from the 2010 Sarah Boxer interview in *The New York Review of Books*, see above.

09 Hedda Sterne in an interview by Anney Bonney, the painter and art writer, in *Bomb* magazine, April 1, 1992.

10 The verbatim exchange from 1981 is as follows: Interviewer S.L. Sanger: "I was curious if you had any particular—if anybody took note of the fact that you were a woman. Did you have any problems, I mean, or were you treated differently?" Libby: "That's a dumb thing to say! I'm going to make a phone call." The audio is online at soundcloud.com/atomicheritage/leona-marshall-libby.

11 Marshall tells this story about finding her graduate advisor in her 1979 memoir, *The Uranium People*.

12 Des Jardins writes about several women scientists and how they navigated patriarchy in her book, *The Madame Curie Complex* (Feminist Press, 2010).

13 From science writer Marguerite Holloway's article, "Finding the Good in the Bad: A Profile of Rita Levi-Montalcini," originally published in *Scientific American* in 1993 and republished December 30, 2012.

14 From *Outside There, Somewhere!*, Kallen's 1964 feminist comic novel, which was republished in the UK in 1973 under the title *Gentlemen Prefer Slaves*.

15 Sunny Parich conducted the interview on April 25, 1998 for the Television Academy Foundation's archive, "The Interviews: An Oral History of Television."

16 From the same Television Academy Foundation's 1998 Oral History interview, see above.

17 Reported in the *Daily Mail*, October 5, 1942, as quoted by Matt Perry in his book, *'Red Ellen' Wilkinson: Her Ideas, Movements and World*, (Manchester University Press, 2015).

18 Rich Slatta, Professor Emeritus of History, North Carolina State University, gave his opinion in a 2021 email to the author.

19 The National Cowboy & Western Heritage Museum is located in Oklahoma City, Oklahoma, USA.

20 Mary Lou LeCompte, "Home on the Range: Women in Professional Rodeo: 1929–1947," in the *Journal of Sport History*, University of Illinois Press, Winter, 1990.

21 The Icelandic Women's History Archives is an excellent source for the fascinating stories of Laufey and her mother: kvennasogusafn.is/index.php?page=laufey-valdimarsdottir

22 From Colette's novel *The Last of Chéri*, (Calmann-Lévy, Paris, 1926)

23 Sarraute's words about Beckett are found in the book *Beckett Remembering Remembering Beckett*, edited by James and Elizabeth Knowlson (Arcade, 2006).

24 Excerpt from *Tropisms* (New Directions, 2015). Originally published in 1939, *Tropisms* was reissued by Les Editions de Minuit in 1957, and translated into English by Maris Jolas (1963, Calder).

25 Anna Cooper, the Black educator and scholar, was born enslaved and earned her PhD from the Sorbonne in Paris. Her ground-breaking book, *A Voice from the South*, was published in 1892, so our young student may have read it at some point in her studies or subsequent career.

26 The line was her riposte to her friend Jean Cocteau, to end an argument. As cited by Wallace Fowlie, in his book, *Jean Cocteau: The History of a Poet's Age*, in Chapter 2, "The Poet's Birth 1889–1914," (Indiana, 1966). The book is online as part of the Open Indiana project.

27 Scholar Catherine Perry's description is from her interesting website, annedenoailles.org. Perry wrote the book, *Persephone*

Unbound: Dionysian Aesthetics in the Works of Anna De Noailles, (Bucknell University Press, 2003).

28 From the *Daily News* article published on January 16, 1931: "12 Bandit Suspects, Alleged 'Gun Molls' Go On Trial Jan 20".

29 Kahn Breton's sleep text, "This took place in springtime…" is quoted and translated on page 17 of the book, *Surrealist Women, An International Anthology*, edited by Penelope Rosemont, (Athlone Press, 1998).

30 Chalifoux's comments from 1974 were quoted in her obituary in the *Plain Dealer*, August 1, 2008.

31 As above.

32 From an interview with Stark by K. Linda Kivi for the 1992 book *Canadian Women Making Music*, cited by Philip Fine in "She Knew the Score for Women in Music," his article in *The Globe and Mail*, April 3, 2012.

33 Violinist Mary Machin described Stark's leonine behavior in a 1995 *Montreal Gazette* article, quoted by Philip Fine in his article in *The Globe and Mail*, April 3, 2012.

34 Sanabria's words were quoted by Felix Contreras in his April 8, 2010 blog post on NPR.org, "Before Celia Cruz Or J.Lo, There Was Graciela".

35 Georg Muche, the first Bauhaus weaving workshop master, is quoted by Sigrid Weltge-Wortmann in her book, *Bauhaus Textiles: Women Artists and the Weaving Workshop* (Thames & Hudson, 1998), according to Geoffrey Bunting in his September 26, 2019 dailyartmagazine.com article, "Frauhaus: Gunta Stölzl, Walter Gropius, and the Women of the Bauhaus."

36 From the article "Jane Campion Talks 'Top of the Lake,' Ignoring 'CSI' Formula," published in *The Hollywood Reporter*, October 9, 2012.

37 From the article, "Jane Campion Thinks It's 'Insane' She's the Only Woman Director to Win Cannes," by Jada Yuan published in *Vulture*, May 26, 2017.

38 From an interview with Jane Campion by Kate Muir published in *The Guardian*, May 20, 2018.

39 "The Werewolf of Washington," a short appreciation of the 2020 director's cut, by critic Richard Brody published in *The New Yorker*.

40 From the article "The prime of Miss Madeline Linford," by Mary Stott, published in *The Guardian*, April 30, 1971.

41 As quoted from the article "The First Page," September 11, 1963, amongst the many selections from her columns posted at madelinelinford.wordpress.com

42 As above.

43 Mary Wollstonecraft, *A Vindication of the Rights of Woman*, chapter 9 (1792).

44 This quip is quoted in *The Unimportance of Being Oscar*, by Oscar Levant (1968).

45 Credible lore attributes this line to Parker, as exhaustively outlined by Quote Investigator: quoteinvestigator.com/2015/11/21/horticulture

46 This quip is quoted by Marion Meade, from her interview with Allen Saalburg, as reported in her 1989 book, *Dorothy Parker: What Fresh Hell Is This?*

47 Dammas' daughter spoke to writer Ted Morgan, who wrote of his efforts to track down the whole jury in his 1975 *Esquire* magazine article, "The Rosenberg Jury: Once They Listened; Now They Talk."

48 From a 1914 speech Perkins gave for a feminist program titled, "Breaking into the Human Race," at Cooper Union in New York City, described by Sandra Adickes in her book, *To Be Young Was Very Heaven:*

Women in New York Before the First World War (Macmillan, 1997).

49 Perkins wrote these words in a 1945 letter to suffragist Carrie Chapman Catt, according to Frances Seeber, in her article, "Eleanor Roosevelt and Women in the New Deal: A Network of Friends," published in *Presidential Studies Quarterly*, 1990.

50 This line, "In the beginning, woman was truly the sun" is by Hiratsuka Raichō and opened the first edition of *Seitō* (bluestocking), a woman's journal founded in Tokyo in 1911. Hiratsuka Raichō and Komako Kimura were feminists of the same age but different class backgrounds; they did not work together.

51 Kimura was interviewed for a 1917 article in *The Woman Citizen*, an American feminist newspaper.

52 In his essay, "The Queen of the Quagmire," published in *The New York Review of Books*, October 25, 2007, the writer and politician Rory Stewart, considers three biographies, her own work, and an archival project on Bell.

53 Rory Stewart, in the essay cited above, quotes from a 1920 letter by Bell.

54 Latife Hanım's family has declined to release her private papers even after the expiration of a 25-year court-ordered ban. "Veil Remains over Atatürk Marriage," by Helena Smith in *The Guardian*, March 7, 2005.

55 *Madam Atatürk*, a biography by İpek Çalişlar, is available in an English translation and reviewed by Melanie Ho in *The Asian Review of Books*, October 18, 2019, and includes more about the couple's mutual attraction and conflict.

56 For more about the relationship, including the conflict about drinking, and the ill-fated reception and its fall-out, see "Latife Hanım: More Than Just the Wife of Atatürk," an article by Ayşe

Kardaş in online publication, *Daily Sabah*, September 8, 2014.

57 For a good brief source on the Bund, including *doykeyt*, (or *doikayt*) see: yivoencyclopedia.org/article.aspx/Bund

58 The description of the conference draws from the article, "World Socialists Convene in Vienna," by John MacCormac, in the *New York Times*, July 26, 1931.

59 See "Female Empowerment? One Woman and 19 Men in Abe's Cabinet," by Rieko Miki, Oct. 3, 2018 post on asia.nikkei.com

60 From the article "Japanese women struggle to have a voice in politics," by Julian Ryall, May 10, 2018 on dw.com

61 Dikaia Chatziefstathiou, in her article, "Reading Baron Pierre de Coubertin: Issues of Gender and Race" published in *Aethlon: The Journal of Sport Literature* (Spring/Summer 2008 edition), quotes Pierre de Coubertin's judgment, which was published in the book, *Pierre de Coubertin 1863-1937 – Olympism: Selected Writings*, in his article "The Women at the Olympic Games."

62 Switzer's descriptions of that day are all drawn from her 2007 memoir *Marathon Woman*. She has posted excerpts on her website kathrineswitzer.com/1967-boston-marathon-the-real-story

63 As above from Switzer's memoir.

64 As above from Switzer's memoir.

65 The full text of Cummings' poem can be found online at the poetrynook.com

66 This history draws from the article, *"No Unescorted Ladies Will Be Served,"* in the online magazine *JSTOR Daily*, by Sascha Cohen, March 20, 2019.

67 All quotes by Chisholm are drawn from her 1970 memoir, *Unbought and Unbossed*.

68 Shola Lynch made the 2005 documentary, *CHISHOLM '72: Unbought & Unbossed*, and wrote the introduction to the fortieth anniversary edition of Chisholm's book n(Take Root Media, 2010).

69 Also from *Unbought and Unbossed*.

70 From an interview with Smith by Zoe Whitley in *The White Review*, March 2021.

71 Smith is quoted in "She Took Photos Of New York Culture for Decades. Now She's Getting Her Due," an article in *Buzzfeed News*, by Pia Peterson, November 14, 2021.

72 From a conversation between Smith and the artist Arthur Jafa, for the *Dreamweavers* series, posted on YouTube.

73 From Anny Shaw's article, "Ming Smith: 'Being a Black Woman Photographer Was Like Being Nobody'," published in the *Financial Times*, September 26, 2019.

74 Smith's observation about making something out of nothing, comes in the article in *Buzzfeed News*, by Pia Peterson, November 14, 2021.

75 From the article "First Woman in Space Dreams of Flying to Mars," published by *Reuters*, March 6, 2007.

76 From the article, "Betsy Wade," by Emma Rothberg, for the National Women's History Museum website: womenshistory.org/education-resources/biographies/betsy-wade

77 From a 2021 email interview with the author.

78 From a 2021 email interview with the author.

79 The story is told in "Marion Carpenter, 82; '40s News Photographer Died in Obscurity," an unbylined obituary in the *Los Angeles Times*, November 29, 2002.

80 Biographical details and the St. Paul Camera Club award from Wikipedia's excellent entry: en.wikipedia.org/wiki/Marion_Carpenter

81 From *Christine Jorgensen: a Personal Autobiography* (Bantam, 1968).

82 The reference to the style inspiration was published in *Variety*, in Ramin Setoodeh's article: "'The Devil Wears Prada' Turns 10: Meryl Streep, Anne Hathaway and Emily Blunt Tell All," June 23, 2016.

83 The lyrics from "Downhearted Blues" are quoted in "How Bessie Smith Influenced A Century Of Popular Music," an essay by Maureen Mahon, published by NPR, August 5, 2019.

84 The influence of the song "Crazy Blues" is discussed in "A Song That Changed Music Forever," an essay by David Hajdu published in the *New York Times*, August 8, 2020

85 This poetic list of the themes of classic blues songs comes from the subject index to the book *Black Pearls* by black studies scholar Daphne Duval Harrison, as quoted by Angela Davis in her book, *Blues Legacies and Black Feminism: Gertrude 'Ma' Rainey, Bessie Smith, and Billie Holiday*, (Pantheon, 1998). Davis notes that it is revealing that Duval Harrison's list "does not include children, domestic life, husband, and marriage."

86 From the chapter, "I Used to be Your Sweet Mama" in Angela Davis' book cited above.

87 See, for example, Mahon's essay cited above, "How Bessie Smith Influenced a Century Of Popular Music."

88 Li Yuhang, Associate Professor of Chinese Art at the University of Wisconsin-Madison, discusses her groundbreaking research on Cixi's agency in a 2021 videotaped talk and in the paper, "Oneself as a Female Deity: Representations of Empress Dowager Cixi as Guanyin,".

89 Benjamin's remark is quoted by

Carol Brown, in her 1985 dissertation, "Ethel Benjamin, New Zealand's First Woman Lawyer," University of Otago available at hdl.handle.net

90 Benjamin's speech is from Janet November's book, *In the Footsteps of Ethel Benjamin: New Zealand's First Woman Lawyer*. (Victoria University Press, 2009).

91 From a *Santa Ana Register* article, "Employ Woman as Officer on Anaheim Force," August 22, 1925

92 Alexander Alekhine's assessment of Vera Menchik's talent for the *New York Times* is featured in selections posted at chesshistory.com/winter/extra/carlsbad

93 From a 1943 letter Menchik wrote to *Chess Magazine*, as quoted by Michael S. Rosenwald in his article, "The Forgotten Female Chess Star who Beat Men 90 Years Before 'Queen's Gambit'," in the *Washington Post*, November 28, 2020.

94 From Virginia Wolfe's essay, "A Room of her Own" in which she states: "For my belief is that if we … have five hundred a year and rooms of our own; if we have the habit of freedom and the courage to write exactly what we think; if we escape a little from the common sitting-room and see human beings not always in their relation to each other but in relation to reality; and the sky too, and the trees or whatever it may be in themselves; if we look past Milton's bogey, for no human being should shut out the view; if we face the fact, for it is a fact, that there is no arm to cling to, but that we go alone and that our relation is to the world of reality and not only to the world of men and women, then the opportunity will come and the dead poet who was Shakespeare's sister will put on the body which she has so often laid down."

End notes

95 From the Betty Cuningham Gallery website for Westerlund Roosen's 2017 exhibition.

96 From "Beauties and Beasts: A Conversation with Mia Westerlund Roosen," by Lilly Wei, published in *Sculpture Magazine*, September 2014.

97 As above.

98 From an article by Emily Newburger, "A Class Unto Themselves," published on the Harvard Law Today website, July 1, 2003: today.law.harvard.edu/feature/class-unto

99 These discoveries are from Robert Clarke's biography, *Ellen Swallow: The Woman Who Founded Ecology*, (1973, Follett); as cited in the Decemeber 18, 2018 *Smithsonian Magazine* article by Leila McNeill, "*The First Female Student at MIT Started an All-Women Chemistry Lab and Fought for Food Safety.*"

100 The words of a witness are quoted by her biographer Robert Clarke (1973), as cited by McNeill in the *Smithsonian Magazine* (2018.) See also two more recent works that seek to excavate Swallow's story: *The Remarkable Life and Career of Ellen Swallow Richards* by Swallow, P.C. (John Wiley & Sons, 2014); and *Rachel Carson and her Sisters: Extraordinary Women Who Have Shaped America's Environment* by R.K. Musil, (Rutgers University Press, 2014).

101 "Dangerous animal" are Swallow's words from her diary, quoted by Sasha Chapman in her article "The Woman Who Gave Us the Science of Normal Life," in the online science magazine Nautil.us, from March 30, 2017. See also Francis E. Wylie, in his article "Ellen Swallow Richards: The First Oekologist," first published in 1976 by the *New England Galaxy*, Old Sturbridge Village, and posted by The Jamaica Plain Historical Society website (jphs.org) in 2005.

102 Doctor Lori Wilson, from a telephone interview with the author for this book in 2021.

103 As above.

104 As above.

105 Taken from the Getty Images caption listing for the photo. The full caption runs as follows: "America's Only Woman Fight Promoter and Manager. Miss Florence North of New York, with the members of her pugilistic stable. They are from left to right, Ned Pincus, Al Cliar, Miss North, Charles Picker, Tony Marto and Trainer Jack Fleming. Miss North is the first of her sex to undertake the management of a stable of fighters, and the leather pushers she is shown with here, do their darndest in every bout, for a woman's tongue is a thing of fury."

106 Zelda's essay, "Eulogy on the Flapper," was published in *Metropolitan Magazine*, in June 1922

107 North was quoted in an article titled, "*Woman's Day* [magazine], Says Girl Sleuth Charging Men Bungled Hall Case," in the *Perth Amboy Evening News*, October 18, 1922.

108 In an email interview with the author in 2021, Guthrie wrote: "the thing about top-level auto racing (Indy cars and NASCAR) is that it is very, very expensive. I believe that capable women drivers still have more difficulty finding sponsorship than men do. I said years ago that what the sport really needs is a woman who has all that it takes to succeed in motorsport, and her own fortune as well."

109 From the article "NASCAR's First Female Phenom: Janet Guthrie," by Bert Wilber, February 20, 2010, published on the Bleacher Report website.

110 All remarks by Andrea Motley Crabtree are drawn from a 2021 telephone interview with the author.

111 From the 1930 Federal Census records for Washington State, accessed through ancestry.com

112 Her 1969 interview quote is cited in "New Exhibition Reveals the Feminist Journey of *Washington Post* Publisher Katharine Graham," June 30, 2021 from an article by Julianne McShane, for womensmediacenter.com. A good short source about her feminist journey, is from Katharine Graham's essay, "An Unaccustomed Seat at the Table," in the January 28, 1997 issue of *The Washington Post*. She also wrote a well-received autobiography, and has been portrayed by Meryl Streep in the 2017 film, *The Post*.

113 From Graham's Pulitzer Prize-winning autobiography, *Personal History* (Knopf, 1997).

114 Dominic Sandbrook, in his April 9, 2013 article, "Viewpoint: What if Margaret Thatcher Had Never Been?" for the *BBC News Magazine*, wrote: "... in the summer of 1970, a week after their local MP had joined the cabinet for the first time, the *Finchley Press* sent a journalist to interview her. Did she, he wondered, fancy a crack at becoming Britain's first woman Prime Minister? 'No,' Margaret Thatcher said emphatically. 'There will not be a woman Prime Minister in my lifetime – the male population is too prejudiced.'"

115 This quote is from Thatcher's May 20, 1965 speech to the National Union of Townswomen's Guilds Conference, "Woman – No Longer a Satellite," as reported in the *Evening News*, according to the Margaret Thatcher Foundation website: margaretthatcher.org/document/101374

116 *The Daily Star* article is reproduced and quoted by Kevin Plummer in his October 18, 2014 article, "She Certainly Doesn't Play like a Girl," online at: torontoist.com/2014/10/historicist-she-certainly-doesnt-play-like-a-girl

117 All the comments from Sarah Fuller are from a 2021 telephone interview with the author.

118 The article "The Girl in 'Iron Pajamas' Defies the 'Ghost' of the Spanish Gold", was first published in *The Hamilton Evening Journal* article on June 7, 1924, and is posted on the website treasurenet.com/threads/1922-newspaper-article-about-the-almirante-de-forencia.81334

119 This warning was published in *The Indianapolis Times*, March 26, 1926.

120 David Ward, in his article, "Sunny Lowry," published in *The Guardian*, February 26, 2008, tells the story of Lowry's 2003 visit to her childhood school, when she "recalled that the school had not always been so happy about her swimming ability: "[The headmistress] was a rather stern woman and she looked at me from over her half-moon glasses and said 'Lowry, what is your ambition?' I replied immediately, 'To swim the Channel', and she said, without another word, 'Dismissed.' "

121 From BBC Radio's, *Woman's Hour* program, where the 92-year old Lowry "joins Rebecca Davies to recall her epic swim.": bbc.co.uk/radio4/womanshour/2003_34_fri_03

122 Morgan is quoted in the article "Tracking Down JoAnn Morgan, a Semi-Hidden Figure of U.S. Space History," by David Kamp, published in *Vanity Fair*, December 10, 2018.

123 From the article "The Apollo Engineer Who Almost Wasn't Allowed in the Control Room," by Marina Koren and published in *The Atlantic*, July 19, 2019.

124 Dunbar's memories are all drawn from the oral history by J. Trova Heffernan and Lori Larson: *An Adventurous Mind, Bonnie Dunbar: The Oral History of Washington's First Woman Astronaut*, conducted for the Washington State Heritage Center, Legacy Project, Office of the Secretary of State, 2009, Olympia, Washington.

125 This account of the British Association gathering, by R.D. 'O Good and A. B. Rendle, appeared in the *Journal of Botany* volume 63 (1925).

126 From the book, *The History of Imperial College London, 1907–2007*, by Hannah Gay.

127 From Hayden Herrera's important 1983 book, *Frida: A Biography of Frida Kahlo*.

128 From a letter to Rosamond Lehmann, written in 1958 when Gellhorn was fifty. The letter is quoted by Fintan O'Toole in his essay, "A Moral Witness," in the October 8, 2020 edition of *The New York Review of Books*, about Gellhorn and the volume of her collected letters, *Yours, for Probably Always: Martha Gellhorn's Letters of Love and War, 1930–1949*, edited by Janet Somerville.

129 Gellhorn was the only woman who landed with the troops in the D-Day morning invasion. There were nurses working on the nursing ship who did not immediately disembark, and other women who got to the front lines, who were already in France or came later. See, for example: "D-Day: 150,000 Men – and One Woman," by Martha Burk, published in the *Huffington Post*, June 5, 2014, and updated December 6, 2017.

130 This claim comes from Fintan O'Toole, who writes: "Sexual connection eluded her. She wrote to Allen Grover from Paris in 1936 of her female friends' diagnosis: 'They are now decided that I am a lesbian because no men mar

the scenery, because I deny the gloating satisfaction in physical love whereof they all brag'." In that letter of 1934, her husband de Jouvenel calls himself "half-a-man and you half-a-woman" because she did not share his sexual pleasure in their couplings. He blamed himself for the "violent physical incompatibility" that existed between them, and called himself an "incompetent lover." But Gellhorn clearly felt the failure to be her own. She told him she was "going to see a doctor about my lack of sexual reaction." She wrote to him of how I failed you, being unable to give you complete joy in sexual love—because I was unable to attain that climax; and how I even faked it on occasions when you had tried and I felt your wretchedness at failure."

131 The cable from Cuba is quoted in Fintan O'Toole's article cited above.

132 O'Toole quotes these moving words from Gellhorn's mother, which he draws from what he refers to as "Somerville's invigorating collection" of Gellhorn's letters.

133 Fascinating oral histories with several women who undertook war jobs on the Pennsylvania Railroad were conducted by Robert Lukens in 1998. The recordings are available at the Hagley Museum and Library's digital archive at digital.hagley.org/AUD_1998234_B01_ID03. Transcription by the author.

134 Kay Dworchak was also recorded in 1998 by Robert Lukens, see above.

135 Quoted by Keith L. Alexander on December 11, 2020 in the Washington Post, in his article, "Gloria Richardson Pushed Aside a Bayonet as a '60s Civil Rights Activist. Now 98, she wants the New Generation to Fight On."

136 Richardson's comments on the moment portrayed in the photo are also drawn from Alexander's 2020 Washington Post article, see above.

137 Richardson said in a news conference at the time: "A first-class citizen does not plead to the white power structure to give him something that the whites have no power to give or take away. Human rights are human rights, not white rights." She was talking about why she refused to ask Black residents of Cambridge to vote on the so-called Treaty of Cambridge that had been negotiated to bring a stop to street protests in the town. Her position angered Robert F. Kennedy and some Black leaders who had worked on the negotiation.

138 Richardson tells the story of Kennedy asking if she knew how to smile in Alexander's Washington Post article.

139 Richardson made these comments on the 1963 March on Washington during her August 27, 2013 appearance on Amy Goodman's television program Democracy Now!, which marked the fiftieth anniversary of the March.

140 As above.

141 Richardson's warning is from Alexander's Washington Post article.

142 This childhood story is recounted in an article by Parvathi Menon, "Captain Lakshmi Sahgal (1914–2012) – A Life of Struggle," published in The Hindu, July 23, 2012, and updated July 05, 2016.

143 McCready's comment comes from her brief appearance at the end of a videotaped 2012 panel interview, "Birth of the Civil Rights Movement in Maryland," which is posted on CSPAN at c.span.org/video/?304562-1/birth-civil-rights-movement-maryland

144 From the opening of Florence Nightingale's 1860 book, Notes on Nursing.

145 This pronouncement by Ramos was recounted by a friend at her funeral, as reported in "Ángela Ramos: la primera reportera peruana," by Natalia Lizama, May 26, 2021, in El Comercio.

146 This passage from Ramos' first column is quoted in "Ángela Ramos Relayze escritora política de Perú," by Hortensia Hernández, February 23, 2019 on the website heroinas.net/2019/02/angela-ramos-relayze-escritora-politica

147 Maurice Casey, who works from Dublin, shared his research in an email exchange with the author. Researching the life stories and interconnections of these itinerant women revolutionary workers is a fascinating new avenue to historical understanding.

148 McInroy's memories and comments throughout are all drawn from a phone interview she gave to the author in 2021.

149 Clarke in a 1983 videotaped interview by Kinny Littlefield, in the author's archive.

150 Clarke in a 1983 profile for National Public Radio, by Liz Roberts.

151 Hogg recounted this story in 2021, in an email interview with the author.

152 From "Pre-Raphaelite Women: Images of Femininity," by Jan Marsh (1987, New York: Harmony Books), quoted in the Wikipedia entry for Jane Morris: en.wikipedia.org/wiki/Jane_Morris

153 Quoted by Nicola Davison in her article, "May Morris, the Overlooked Star of the Arts and Crafts Movement," from the November 10, 2017 issue of the Financial Times.

154 Rowan Bain's comment is from the same source as noted above.

155 As above.

156 From the article "Woman in the News; Daughter of Determination: Benazir Bhutto," by Barbara Crosset, published on December 2, 1988 in the New York Times.

157 Amy Wilentz's remarkable essay, "Benazir Bhutto: A Killing and Three Funerals," in the Huffington Post, December 28, 2007, and updated on May 25, 2011.

158 As reported in People Magazine, "The Secrets of France's Super Chef, Paul Bocuse: Cook Quicker Than the Concorde and Butter Up the World," September 6, 1976, by Rudi Chelminski.

159 As quoted by the Bocuse d'Or organization on its own website: bocusedor-winners.com/uk/chefs/liste-chef/linster,8

160 From Pickford's 1955 autobiography, Sunshine and Shadow (Doubleday).

161 From a 2021 email interview between the author and Cari Beauchamp, who serves the Mary Pickford Foundation as resident scholar.

162 From Cari Beauchamp's book, Without Lying Down: Frances Marion and the Powerful Women of Early Hollywood, (Scribner, 1997).

163 From "That's Me in the Picture: Ninalee Craig Photographed by Ruth Orkin in Florence in 1951, aged 23," as interviewed by Abigail Radnor, in The Guardian, January 30, 2015.

164 Evans' wish was expressed in the article, "2 Years After Going Viral, Ieshia Evans Reflects on Her Iconic Protest Photo," by Ja'han Jones in the Huffington Post, July 5, 2018, and updated July 6, 2018.

165 From an excellent six-minute video about Evans, in a BBC story made by Anna Bressanin in 2016: bbc.com/news/av/magazine-38028755

166 These closing thoughts from Evans are also from the 2018 Huffington Post article.

Index

Picture credits

agefotostock / © JMH / Galaxy Contact / Spacephotos: 171, 227bcr; akg-images: 59, 223bl; Alamy Stock Photo: / Chronicle: 33, 221bl, / CPA Media Pte Ltd: 129, 221bcl, / Matteo Omied: 187, 224bcr; Courtesy Anaheim Public Library: 133, 223bcl; ANNO/Austrian National Library/ Neue Wiener Schachzeitung, 1929, no. 16, page 243: 135, 223tc; All rights reserved © Copyright – ANSA: 27, 228br; © Bocuse d'Or: 209, 229bc; Boston City Hospital Collection, 7020.001, City of Boston Archives, Boston: 191, 220tcl; Bridgeman Images / © Mario Dondero: 39, 226bcr, / Galerie Bilderwelt: 179, 223tcr; Courtesy Castelli Gallery, New York / © 1991 Hans Namuth Estate. Courtesy Center for Creative Photography: 141, 228tr; Cino del Duca/RGA: 13R; City of Vancouver Archives: 114–115, 225tc; Courtesy of The Cleveland Orchestra / Photo by Geoffrey Landesman, 1934: 53, 225tcl; Andrea Motley Crabtree: 155, 228bcr; Dover Museum and Bronze Age Boat Galley/Audrey Scott Collection: 169, 226tr; Linn M. Ehrlich: 197, 227tr; Eyevine/Walter Doughty/ Guardian: 67, 222bcl, / © NYT: 109, 228tcl, / © Barton Silverman / © NYT: 101, 227br, Yin Bogu/Xinhua: 6; Getty Images: 97, 221tcr, / Afro American Newspapers / Gado: 14, / Anthony Barboza: 127, 222bl, / Bettmann: 69, 71, 77, 99, 103, 119, 151, 167, 221tr, 222bc, 222br, 224tc, 225tcr, 226tcl, 227bc, 228tl, / Corbis: 23, 225bcl, / Evening Standard / Stringer: 111, 227bcl, / Fox Photos / Stringer: 31, 224tcl, / General Photographic Agency / Hulton Deutsch: 79, 215, 222tcl, 225tl, / Historical Picture Archive: 205, 220bcl, / Photo by © Hulton-Deutsch Collection/CORBIS/

Corbis: 83, 223br, / John Byrne Cooke Estate: 65, 227tcr, / John Springer Collection / Corbis: 13C, / JP Jazz Archive: 51, 222bcr, / Keystone-France: 37, 224bl, / Keystone / Stringer: 161, 228bc, / Dan Kitwood: 12r, / Kyodo News: 89, 229bcr, / NBC: 29, 226tc, / New York Daily News Archive: 47, 121, 223tr, 226bc, / Pool Benainous/ Hounsfield/Legrand: 63, 229tc, / Popperfoto: 93, 224bc, / San Francisco Chronicle/Hearst Newspapers: 117, 227tc, / Science and Society Picture Library: 25, 221bc, / Ian Tryas / Stringer: 123, 228tcr; Harvard Law School Library, Historical & Special Collections / Martin J. Paul: 145, 229tl; Hoover Institution Library & Archives, Stanford University: 195, 222tcr© IWM: 181, 224br; © Matthew R Lewis, courtesy of Andrew Shanahan, Matthew R Lewis Estate, matthewrlewisportraits. co.uk: 201, 229bcl; Library and Archives Canada / Ethel Stark fonds/5667882/ Photographer: J.P. Laliberté: 55, 225bc; Library of Congress, https://www. loc.gov/item/00651765: 43, 220tcr, /2007664642/: 10–11, /2016804774/: 91, 220tc, /photograph by Harris & Ewing, 2016875186/: 73, 224tcr, item/98519364/): 41, 220tl, / William P. Gottlieb/Ira and Leonore S. Gershwin Fund Collection, Music Division: 57, 225bcr; London School of Tropical Medicine, 71st Session. Wellcome Collection. Attribution 4.0 International (CC BY 4.0): 9r; Mairie de Bordeaux, Musée des Beaux-Arts, photo L. Gauthier: 13l; Mary Evans: / © The Illustrated London News: 139, 224tl; Mary Pickford Foundation: 211, 223tcl; Courtesy of the Maryland Center for History and Culture / Library, Special Collections, Paul S. Henderson Photograph Collection, RS6597 [HEN.02.07-019]: 189, 225br; © McCord Museum / Wm Notman & Son: 143, 222tl; Courtesy MIT Museum: 147, 220bcr; National Air and Space Museum - Smithsonian Institution:

107, 227bl; National Museum of the American Indian, Smithsonian Institution P15389. Photo by NMAI Photo Services: 87, 220bl; National Museum of Iceland: 35, 221tc; Copyright 1952, 1980 Ruth Orkin: 213, 226bl; © Peyo – 2022 - Licensed through I.M.P.S. (Brussels) – www.smurf.com: 12l; Reuters / Jonathan Bachman: 217, 229tcr, / Kim Kyung-Hoon: 125, 229tr, / George Walker IV-USA TODAY NETWORK: 165, 229br; ©The Royal Society: 175, 223tl; Photo Scala, Florence: / © 2022. / Photothèque R. Magritte/Adagio Images, Paris, / SCALA, Florence / © ADAGP, Paris and DACS, London 2022: 15/ RMN-Grand Palais /Dist.: 113, 203, 220br, 221tl, / Purchase, with funds from the Jack E. Chachkes Endowed Purchase Fund. Inv.: 2020.55. New York, Whitney Museum of American Art. Digital image Whitney Museum of American Art / Licensed by Scala / Anthony Barboza photographer: 105, 228bl; Schlesinger Library, Harvard Radcliffe Institute: 182, 224tr; / © The Estate of Bettye Lane: 153, 228tc; / FayFoto Boston: 75, 226bcl; Science Photo Library: / NASA: 173, 229bl; Scurlock Studio Records, Archives Center, National Museum of American History, Smithsonian Institution: 137, 149, 224bcl, 226br; Shutterstock / AP: 159, 185, 227tcl, 228bcl, /Malcolm Clarke/ANL: 207, 229tcl, Ian Langsdon/ EPA: 7, / Nina Leen / The LIFE Picture Collection: 21, 226tl; Image: Telimage, Paris / © Man Ray 2015 Trust / DACS, London 2022: 49, 222tr; The University of Texas at San Antonio, 084-0592/ General Photograph Collection/UTSA Special Collections: 61, 221bcr; Collection of Toitū Otago Settlers Museum: 131, 221tcl; Margaret Lenz Photographic Collection, Alaska and Polar Regions Collections & Archives, University of Alaska Fairbanks: 157, 220tr; C:22/1/1 Savitar - Courtesy of University Archives, University of Missouri: 19, 220bc; Manuscripts, Archives and Special Collections,

Washington University State Libraries, Grays Harbor Collections/pc170b3p01_ ACGirardmetalworkersAberdeen: 95, 221br;Wellcome Collection: 45, 222tc, / In copyright: 9l, / Public Domain Mark: 8; Courtesy of the Western Regional Archives, State Archives of North Carolina: 177, 225tr; Wikimedia Commons: José Carlos Mariátegui Archive (cc-by-2.0): 193, 223bc; Wisconsin Center for Film and Theater Research, Shirley Clarke Papers: 199, 227tl; Working Class Movement Library: 81, 225bl; From the Archives of the YIVO Institute for Jewish Research, New York: 85, 223bcr; York University Libraries, Clara Thomas Archives & Special Collections, Toronto Telegram fonds, ASC00898: 163, 226tcr

238

Author's Acknowledgments

My mother, Anna Lou Aldrich, was often an Only Woman, and I dedicate this book to her memory. Her friend, the late Joanna Rose, and her beloved husband Dan, who have so kindly supported my work.

Nothing would have happened without Elisa Blatteis Roberts, who pried an early version out of my too-timid hands, sent it out into the world, and stayed by my side all the way. My sisters Alison Humes and Alex Humes Aldrich gave early encouragement, and Alison was exceedingly generous with her sage advice and well-known editorial genius. Tracy Young, Rebecca Friday, and Andy McCord lent their considerable smarts, and dear friends Kara Blake, Ron K. Fried, and Titta Cappabava contributed some of my favorite photographs.

Patricia Soledad Llosa has been a much needed best friend—as have Valerie Goodman, Bella Meyer, Judith Zeitlin, Lamia Balafrej, and other angels I rely on for so much, including responding to polls on photographic preferences. I got ideas and support from Steve Dembitzer, Sarah Maher, Augusta Palmer, Joel Whitney, Lee Warshavsky, John Firestone, Jenny Mascia, Nile Southern, and none from my brother Malcolm Einaudi, who pointed out that the skeletons pictured may have been female, breaking the rules. Yaddo provided space and beauty, where the seeds were planted, as did Nancy Kates.

I am deeply grateful to the wonderful team at Phaidon: my editor Virginia McLeod, Deb Aaronson, Emma Barton, Jenny Faithful, Julia Hasting, and others behind the scenes who worked hard through the pandemic to make it real. And thanks to Bill Van Parys, who hooked us up! My agent William Clarke has been invaluable, with much appreciated patience and good humor. Susan Shulman and Stephanie Steiker also gave good advice at a crucial moment.

Last but not least, it was exhilarating to hear from the Only Women and scholars I was able to reach; they shared their experiences with enthusiasm and generosity.

Publisher's Acknowledgments

The publisher would like to acknowledge the invaluable contributions of the following people: James Brown, Anjali Bulley, Clive Burroughs, Lisa Delgado, Jenny Faithful, Julia Hasting, João Mota, Ana Rita Teodoro and Grace Tran.

Phaidon Press Limited
2 Cooperage Yard
London E15 2QR

Phaidon Press Inc.
65 Bleecker Street
New York, NY 10012

phaidon.com

First published 2022
Reprinted 2023
© 2022 Phaidon Press Limited

ISBN 978 1 83866 420 6

A CIP catalogue record for this book is
available from the British Library and
the Library of Congress.

Commissioning Editor: Virginia McLeod
Project Editor: Emma Barton
Production Controller: Sarah Kramer
Typesetting: Cantina
Design: Julia Hasting

Printed in Hong Kong